Rock On!

By: Adam DeRose

To all the rockers out there,
keep on rolling!

Contents:

Intro

Every story has a beginning. Mine began on Sunday September 1, 1996 in downtown Buffalo. My dad, the Donald, was a docent at the Buffalo and Erie County Naval Park. That Sunday evening, the Naval Park was hosting a Battle of the Bands on the back of the USS Little Rock battleship. I thought it was an awesome concept, a Battle of the Bands on a battleship!

At the young age of 12, that was my first concert! There were about four or five local bands participating in the battle, though I only remember two of the bands. The first band was 53 Days. I remember them because I bummed a CD off of them. They were selling CDs and some other merchandise at their table. I wanted a CD but I told them I didn't have enough money because I was 12 and didn't have a job. They took pity on me...or just wanted to shut me up. After they gave me their album, *Why Would You Care*, I asked each band member if they would autograph the cover, which they did.

The other band that participated in the Battle of the Bands was Johnny Revolting! I was able to bum a 45 record off of Johnny Revolting! The 45, *Continue Revolting!*, had four songs on it, *CYO Dropout* being my favorite cut off the record. I also had the guys of Johnny Revolting! autograph the liner notes.

I remembered that the set changes were long and boring. Since I was too young to consume alcohol or partake in the normal debauchery routines of concerts (sex, drugs & rock-n-roll!), I wandered back to the docent's lounge and watched the Sunday night football game, the Buffalo Bills @ New Jersey Giants. That game, the Bills erased a 20-7 Giants lead, where the Bills came back to win the game in Overtime, 20-23!

That was a very late night for a 12 year old Adam. By the time the Bills game and Battle of the Bands ended, it was well after 11pm! Thankfully I did not have school the next day! There were just a few more days of summer vacation; then it was back to "prison" for 9 months at St. Stephens School.

Having that small taste of going to see live music was awesome. Up until then, I had been raised on the Oldies. There was nothing wrong with the Oldies, but it wasn't my era or generation. I wanted to discover new music, music that didn't suck, music that rocked! This is my journey, my saga, on seeing bands of my youth; when music was new, fresh, and didn't suck! I've decided to tell you about the 27 greatest concerts that I have been to...I figured that 27 was a good Rock-n-Roll number because some of the greatest rockers died at 27. Sit back, relax, crack open a beer, light up that Zippo, and enjoy the show!

Death by Rock!

It was early summer 2003 and the concert season was upon us!

The *BIG TICKET* that summer was the Summer Sanitarium tour featuring Mudvayne, Deftones, Linkin Park, Limp Bizkit with Metallica as headliner! Summer Sanitarium was slated to be at the SkyDome in Toronto on July 5, 2003!

As soon as tickets went on sale, my buddy Mike and I bought ours! Even though the two of us were going, Mike thought it was logical for him to buy four tickets…Mike was never good with math.

In the weeks leading up to the concert, Mike was getting a little nervous because he couldn't find anybody to buy the two additional tickets he bought.

A week before the show, my buddy Jason and Mike's older sister said they would go.

In the days leading up the concert, there was a huge SARS (severe acute respiratory syndrome) epidemic all throughout the GTA (greater Toronto area). According to the Centers for Disease and Control, SARS is a viral respiratory illness caused by a coronavirus. According to "Guy Logic" a Coronavirus is a hangover caused by drinking too many Coronas. And for the record, there would have been no way for me to get the Coronavirus up in Canada because I would only be drinking Canadian beer like Molson!

My father's parents found out that I was headed up to Toronto to see Metallica! Not only were they not Metallica fans, but they did not want me to travel to Toronto with the SARS epidemic going on. I told them, "There's nothing to worry about. And what's the worst that could happen? That I die? Man what a great way to go, at a Metallica concert!" They did not find any humor in it. If I did die at Metallica, I wanted it to be my epitaph on my headstone!

July 5, 2003 finally came. I told Mike that I would drive everyone up to Toronto. My buddy Jason lived next door to me, so he was easy to pick up. Jason and I left South-Central Grand Island late morning. Next we drove to Wheatfield to pick up Mike and his sister; then we headed to the Canadian border.

The drive up to Toronto was boring and uneventful. We had the Toronto rock radio station on and they were broadcasting live from SkyDome. In between songs and commercials, the DJs were giving concert and traffic updates. During our drive up, Mudvayne was playing. The four of us were not Mudvayne fans, so we were not heartbroken to miss their set.

It was mid-afternoon by the time we parked the car in downtown Toronto.

Mike had ordered us some nice seats. Skydome was the home of baseball's Toronto Blue Jays. Our seats were the first row of the upper deck along the foul line of 1st base. The stage was located in the back of the outfield, with fans everywhere on the infield and outfield. Even though the concert was on a hot July 5th, SkyDome's dome was closed. That meant that SkyDome was hot, sticky, and stinky.

By the time we got to our unobstructed seats, the Deftones had taken the stage. I did not like the Deftones. I was hoping to arrive at Skydome late enough to miss them. They played a whole bunch of crap, eventually playing their only decent song, *Change*.

During the set change, Mike and I got up to walk around and find beer. Though Mike and I were only 19, we could legally drink in Canada! The legal drinking age in Ontario was 19, which meant that Mike and I were barely legal! After we got our beer, we found an outdoor landing party deck. Mike and I also bought matching Metallica concert shirts.

Once on the party deck, Mike and I started to people watch. There was a huge line of concert goers waiting to get groped by security. One chick in particular partied a little too hard before she even got into the venue. This chick was so drunk that she literally dropped out of line. Her friends dragged her over to a park bench, where she ended up puking into a flower bed. That's when Mike yelled down to them, "Sex, drugs, and puking!" The friends looked up at Mike and did not find any humor in it, but others in line laughed.

Soon Linkin Park took the stage! Linkin Park was pretty good live, they sounded just like their recorded material. They just came out with their second album *Meteora* earlier that year, so it went without saying that they were going to play songs off the new album like *Numb, Breaking the Habit, Faint Somewhere I Belong* and *Lying From You*. LP also played radio hits, such as *Crawling, In the End,* and *One Step Close*, just to name a few.

After Linkin Park's hour long set, it was time to get some food because Jason and I were starving. All I had to eat that day was an overpriced beer.

Jason and I came upon a Mr. Sub. We waited in line for a long while. Eventually it was time for Jason and me to order our subs. Jason asked for a roast beef sub. He was informed that they were sold out of roast beef. I tried to order a turkey sub and I was told they were out of turkey. Jason and I asked if they had ham or pastrami; they were sold out of those too. Finally Jason and I asked Mr. Sub what they did have. Jason and I ended up buying overpriced vegetable and condiment subs, but since we were starving, it was the best overpriced vegetable condiment sub we ever had!

It felt like each set change was at least an hour long, but eventually Limp Bizkit took the stage! Bizkit was awesome and they played all of their hitz, such as *Re-Arranged, Take a Look Around, Rollin' (Air Raid Vehicle), My Generation,* and other songs. They even covered George Michael's *Faith* and The Who's *Behind Blue Eyes.*

During Limp Bizkit's set, lead singer Fred Durst, wearing his signature red New York Yankees hat, picked out some bitches from the audience to join him on stage while the band played *Nookie.* My favorite part of their set was when the lead guitarist—it wasn't Wes Borland because he had already left the band—jammed out the opening notes to *Break Stuff.* Everyone in Skydome was amped and into the song! Jason, Mike and I felt the upper deck moving beneath us! As the song climaxed to the heavy rock part, I looked down onto the fans on the baseball field. The sea of people jumped and moved around like massive tidal waves with body surfers! Seeing Limp Bizkit live was awesome!

By the time the roadies were finished with their work, it was 10pm. Moments later, the stage lights went out and Metallica's entrance song, *The Ecstasy of Gold*, was played overhead as fans cheered!

Let the head banging begin!

Soon the opening soft notes to *Battery* were heard and diehard fans roared with joy! Metallica built on the fans' energy after *Battery* by playing fan favorites *Master of Puppets, Harvester of Sorrow, Welcome Home (Sanitarium),* and *For Whom the Bell Tolls.*

In between songs, James asked us to welcome the newest member of Metallica, bassist Rob Trujillo. Trujillo replaced long time bassist Jason Newsted.

During Metallica's set, lead singer and rhythm guitarist James Hetfield asked us if we wanted to hear anything off their newest album *St. Anger*. The entire Skydome unanimously shouted back to James, "NO!" James was a little shocked and taken aback. He told us that they were only going to play a song off the new album. Thankfully the set list only contained two songs off the new album, *Frantic* and *St. Anger*.

Metallica slashed out other classics such as *Sad But True, No Remorse, Seek & Destroy,* and *Blackened*.

It seemed like that was it for their set, but they came back out to rock out for an encore! They played one of my favorite songs of theirs, *Fuel*. I liked *Fuel* because it was a hard core car song. Car songs seemed to have gone by the wayside since the Beach Boys and Jan and Dean made them popular in the 1960s. Metallica rounded out their encore with *Nothing Else Matters* and *Creeping Death*.

The sounds of gun fire and heavy attack were heard above the fans cheers. Metallica had surprised us with a second encore. The quiet, soft opening notes of *One* were heard and fans quieted down. As the energy of the song built, so did the fans' enthusiasm and energy!

Metallica ended on a strong note, sending the fans home with a bedtime lullaby, *Enter Sandman*. At the conclusion of *Enter Sandman* Metallica left the stage for good. It was midnight and all the inside lights to Skydome were turned on. I thought the entire show was fucking awesome! I had no complaints about the songs that were played by any band. If anything, I wished that Metallica had a third encore.

Jason, Mike, Mike's sister, and I joined the rat race of fans as we exited the Skydome.

We eventually made our way back to the car. Moments later, we were lost in downtown Toronto and found ourselves driving past a couple post parties. Eventually we found our way to the QEW and back home to Buffalo.

By the time we got home, it was well after 2am and my ear drums were still ringing!

PS-I obviously did not die of SARS because I was able to tell you my account of seeing 'Tallica...or maybe I'm telling it to you from beyond the grave!

Projekt Revolution

The Projekt Revolution tour was hitting Darien Lake Performing Arts Center on July 27, 2004 and my friends and I had tickets.

My buddy Jason and I bought the cheap lawn seats while my buddies Mike and Brian spent more for seats under the awning.

The game plan was for Jason and me to meet up with Brian and Mike. Since Jason lived next door to me, I just walked over to his place when I was ready to leave for the show.

Before Jason and I got to Darien Lake, we needed to pick up some rations of the bubbly hops and barley kind. We stopped at a grocery store in Corfu. I waited in Jason's Jeep while he ran in to get some beer. In America, Jason was of legal age, I was not. I didn't want to run interference, so I kept a low profile and stayed in the Jeep. Minutes later Jason came back with an 18 pack of Labatt Blue.

Once we had beer, we made our way to Darien Lake.

We got to our parking spot early afternoon and began to tailgate. Mike and Brian soon met up with us and the four of us kicked back the brews.

The Projekt Revolution tour had a lot of bands playing, so it was a day long festival at Darien Lake. There were quite a bit of no name opener bands that we did not care to see, which was why we drank in the parking lot.

The four of us finished up our beers in time to make it into the venue to see The Used. I had no interest in seeing them, but Jason did.

After The Used finished their set, it was time for the road crew to swap out the sets. Eventually it was time for Snoop Dogg. Yes, that's right, I said Snoop Dogg. I thought it was a little weird that rapper Snoop Dogg was playing a rock show, but hey, weirder things have happened.

Let's face it, I'm white. I knew who Snoop Dogg was but not his songs.

Snoop was entertaining, especially when he asked for weed…during Snoop's set a huge haze of pot smoke could be clearly seen under the awning of the venue. When Snoop asked for weed between songs, many fans threw their dime bags and Ziploc baggies full of weed up onto the stage. Snoop picked up one of the bags, took some dope out, walked towards the back of the stage, and smoked up; to many fans' delight!

Eventually Snoop Dogg's set was over and he and his posse left the stage to smoke more weed in the tour bus.

Mike, Brian, Jason, and I hung out on the lawn while we waited for Korn. To kill some time we grabbed a round of overpriced beer.

After getting beer, we walked back into the lawn section. There was a fence that segregated the lawn section from the seats under the awning. Since there weren't many people standing by the fence, we all walked up and parked it right there. From our vantage point we had a great, unobstructed view of the stage.

As we were hanging out by the fence, a whole bunch of us dudes noticed a chick who was sitting on top of her seat in the last row of the awning seats. We all noticed her because from behind, she looked hot, especially because her jeans shot down her butt and the whale tail from her thong rode up her back! *Boing!*

I don't really remember whose idea it was, but about 10 of us guys started throwing our change towards the chick's dumper. We were trying to sink a coin down the whale tail and into her butt crack. It was like a fine game of beer pong. The chick sat probably 20-25 feet away from us, at a 10^0 downward angle.

At one point, there were probably 15 guys tossing their change, trying to sink the whale tail!

It was yours truly, with a nickel that sank the shot from downtown! All the dudes cheered! The chick obviously felt something hit her back and travel down into her crack. We thought it was hot when she went grabbing into her ass. Apparently all of us guys were making too much noise because once the chick found the nickel; she turned around to look at us. All nonchalant, all of us guys stopped laughing, looked around, twiddled our thumbs, and whistled as if nothing happened.

Finally the moment was upon us! It was time for Korn!

As soon as Korn took to the stage, the fans cheered and the energy could be felt, quite literally. All the fans on the lawns rushed towards the fence of the lawn section. Brian, Mike, Jason, and I were pinned against the fence. We were amazed with all the force on the fence that it didn't give out.

Korn was touring in support of their latest soon to be released album, *Greatest Hits Vol. 1*. I'll admit it—I felt old! Bands that I had grown up listening to were now churning out greatest hits albums. With that being said, Korn's set was pretty much a greatest hits show, which we had no problem with.

Korn got the mosh pit party started with the head banging and bass heavy sounding song *Right Now*. After hearing *Right Now* it got me in the mood to fuck someone up!

The band kept the anger and rage going with such angst songs as *Blind, Here To Stay, Y'All Want a Single, Somebody Someone, Did My Time,* and *Twist*. And how could they forget fan favorite *A.D.I.D.A.S.*? Fans were thrilled to hear *A.D.I.D.A.S.* and showed it by singing along! Honestly, who doesn't dream about sex all day? On Korn's *Greatest Hits Vol. 1*, there are covers of Cameo's *Word Up* and Pink Floyd's *Another Brick in the Wall (Parts 1,2,3)* which to the delight of fans they played. Of course lead singer Jonathan Davis came out with bag pipes to play the intro to *Shoots and Ladders*. No Korn concert would be complete without hearing *Got the Life, Falling Away from Me,* and *Freak on a Leash*.

Korn was spectacular live! Korn and the fans fed off each other's energy and it showed with all the mosh pits and crowd surfers!

By the time Korn finished performing, it was dark and we had one last band to see, Linkin Park! Brian and Mike parted ways with Jason and me and went to find their seats under the awning for Linkin Park.

After the hour long set change, it was finally time for Linkin Park to take the stage!

Linkin Park's energy level was off the charts; they picked up right from where Korn left off!

Linkin Park was still touring in support of their second album *Meteora*. LP's stage show left Jason and me blind because they had a lot of strobe lights going off.

Linkin Park rocked out tunes *Lying From You, Somewhere I Belong,* and *Faint*.

During Linkin Park's set Jason and I got tired of getting smothered by a barrage of crowd surfers. By the fifth time of getting kicked in the head by a crowd surfer, we had had it. Instead of letting the surfer down nicely, we tossed the surfer right over the fence and he rolled down the embankment and into the legs of security. Security picked up the guy and hauled his ass out.

Lead singer Chester Bennington and backing vocalist Mike Shinoda belted out vocals for *Numb*, *Breaking the Habit*, *Crawling*, and *In the End*.

When it seemed like they were done, they came back out for an encore. Joining LP for their last song was Korn's lead guy Jonathan Davis to help on vocals for *One Step Closer*. After the show, Jason and I waited forever in Darien Lake traffic. Eventually we made it back to Buffalo, where we had Mighty Taco for a late dinner, and then home for bed.

Mommy, Where's Fluffy?

It was Sunday October 10, 2004 and the *Madly in Anger with the World Tour* featuring Godsmack and Metallica was in Buffalo. More importantly, my buddy Mike and I had floor level tickets for the concert!

Before Mike and his buddy Kyle picked me up for the show, I decided to pregame. I had a couple nips of Jose Cuervo to get me primed for the show.

Once we got downtown and Kyle parked his Pontiac Grand Prix (pronounced prick), we met up with a couple of Mike's buddies because they were able to score us some beer! Mike and I weren't 21 yet, so we still needed sources to get us beer. Mike's friend could only score us a couple cans of Labatts.

After we polished off the cans of beer, Mike remembered that his other buddy, Shades, had a keg of beer. Shades was a DJ on Buffalo's rock station. Mike and I walked all cool like and met up with him underneath the Skyway. There were a bunch of people with solo cups hanging around the keg. Eventually someone got the great idea to do keg stands! Mike and I got in line to do keg stands. Mike was on deck, ready to walk up to the keg when someone asked him if he was 21. As opposed to saying "yes" Mike said, "Well, I'm turning 21 in December." The MC of the keg stands looked at Mike and said, "Well you're not 21, so you can't do it."

Not being a dumbass, I walked up to the keg and said, "Yeah, I'm 21! Let's do this!" Mike looked jealous.

Seconds later, I was grabbing the keg as two dudes hoisted my legs into the air and over my head. A third guy put the tap in my mouth and asked if I was ready for beer. I shook my head and said, "Fuck yeah! Let's do this!"

I went 17 seconds for my first keg stand and it was awesome!

Mike and I hung out with Shades for a few more minutes. Mike was bummed out that he couldn't do a keg stand and we wanted more beer, so we went with Plan C.

Mike's older sister was going to the show as well and she was already inside the venue, HSBC Arena. Moments later we headed into HSBC Arena and within minutes we met up with her. After Mike and I gave her some money, she came back with two Labatt Blues!

By the time Godsmack came out to play, the Jose Cuervo and beer were kicking in, and I was rocking a "brown out."

From my haze, I think I remember Godsmack playing a few tunes off their first, self-titled album *Godsmack*, of which, I think they played *Moon Baby, Whatever, Keep Away, Time Bomb,* and *Bad Religion.*

Bass notes were thumbed out as an old man's voice was heard over head telling, "You have come here from all over the world because society has no use for you…this place will now be your home…" and Godsmack and their fans jammed out to *Immune.*

I'm not going to lie, during the "brown out" a few of Godsmack's song blended together. It didn't help that their early work was all in the same tune. However one song that always stood out was *Voodoo* and I do remember vividly Godsmack playing *Voodoo.*

During Godsmack's set, we heard the Underground come through and a voice over telling us to "Mind the gap," followed by the opening guitar riffs and drum beats to *Someone in London.*

The previous year (2003), Godsmack released their third album, *Faceless*, so Mike and I were anticipating a lot of songs from their new heavy album! In my drunken stupor, from the new album, I think they played instant classic *Straight out of Line.* I think they may have also played *Faceless, I Stand Alone,* and *Re-Align.*

While I was in my alcohol bliss, I remember that Godsmack did play *Batalla de los Tambores*, better known as "dueling drums!" Lead singer Sully Erna and lead drummer Shannon Larkin had a friendly drum-off battle! I loved it! Mike loved it! Fans loved it!

Godsmack did play their other staples *Awake* and *Trippin.* Their set lasted well over an hour, closer to an hour and a half!

After Godsmack ended, I had to piss like a mofo. Mike and I waited in line forever to take a leak.

Without mission completed, we met back up with his sister so we could replenish our beers.

Soon it was the moment we were waiting for! Mike and I wandered back down to the floor and stood by the Zamboni entrance. Since I was rocking a nice buzz, I figured it was a good time to drunk phone call my new girlfriend Shannon. I did not have a cell phone, so I borrowed Mike's. After leaving a rambling, incoherent message on her dorm phone's answering machine, I was good to go.

Minutes later, the house lights were turned down low and Metallica's opening theme song, *The Ecstasy of Gold*, was being played throughout the speakers in HSBC Arena! Mike and I turned around and looked down the Zamboni entrance. We watched as Metallica ran out of the Zamboni entrance and took the stage, which was located at "center ice." Mike and I thought it was awesome that Lars, Kirk, James, and Rob ran right past us!

Seconds later, faint and long guitar notes became louder and more pronounced; it was the opening to *Blackened.*

Metallica's stage spun around in a circle like a carousel, so that everyone in the arena could see the band play. Mike and I were able to weasel our way right up to the stage!

Metallica played my favorite metal car song, *Fuel*. Then they played my favorite another favorite song of mine, *The Four Horsemen*. The song, *The Four Horsemen*, could be found on Metallica's 1st album *Kill 'Em All*, but Mike and I always found the combo liquor filled shot, "the Four Horsemen", up in Canada. The shot consisted for the "*4 Js*" in a shot; Jack Daniels, Jameson, Johnny Walker, and Jim Bean…liquid burning! I had gotten fucked up plenty a time up at the Wild Mushroom in Niagara Falls, Canada on Four Horsemen!

While we are on the topic of booze, *Allcohilica* played my favorite drinking song, *Whiskey in a Jar*. Mike and I held up our beers and sang along with James as he belted out the vocals to *Whiskey in a Jar*. Though *Whiskey* was a cover song, we still loved it!

Unfortunately 'Tallica wasted some time playing a couple new songs off their new record *St. Anger*. They could have played some other covers or original material, but instead they played new songs *Frantic* and *St. Anger*.

Mike and I were surprised, and ecstatic when we heard Metallica play the opening notes to *Fade to Black*. We had heard through Metallica folk lore that they did not like to play that song in concert because lead man James Hetfield suffered a pyrotechnic injury while performing that song years ago in the early 90s. The opening notes were not a teaser; the band played the whole song, much to the delight of the fans!

17

Metallica continued with a great set by playing awesome shit like *The Unforgiven, The Thing That Should Not Be, Master of Puppets,* and they ended with *Fight Fire with Fire.*

The stage lights went out and stayed off for a bit. Though the lights were off, Mike and I could see that Metallica did not leave the stage. It seemed like they were taking a breather or a staged encore.

Suddenly classical music was played over the speakers; it was the opening notes to *No Leaf Clover.* I was pleasantly surprised that Metallica was playing *No Leaf Clover!* It was a song that I instantly loved during high school (at St. Joseph's Collegiate Institute) when their *S&M* album came out.

Pretty much anything old would be a fan favorite, so Metallica played it safe by playing some tunes off their self-titled album *Metallica,* aka, the Black Album. From the Black Album, they played love ballad *Nothing Else Matters.* Also from that album, they treated us to *Sad But True,* and *Enter Sandman.* They also threw in *One.*

To kick off their second encore, Metallica played *Disposable Heroes.* I had always loved *Disposable Heroes* because it was fast and heavy sounding and needed to be cranked on the stereo which got my blood pumping!

Metallica ended their show with *Seek & Destroy.* Before playing the song, front man James Hetfield asked the lights to be turned on. He said that all show long, all us fans were watching him and the band. He told us that he wanted to watch his fans as they played their last song for us. While Metallica and their fans jammed out to *Seek & Destroy* black balloons were dropped from above. The black balloons had demonic looking faces on them, almost like jack-o-lanterns.

At the end of the show, Lars tossed a couple drum sticks into the crowd. James and Kirk tossed a few guitar picks into the audience too. Mike and I each grabbed a guitar pick off the ground, it was pretty bad ass!

Mike and I met up with Kyle, who drove me home. The concert was bad ass and that's the end of my story.

Supergroup

By 2004, it was quite evident that I would never see Guns-n-Roses or Stone Temple Pilots live in concert unless I had some sort of magical DeLorean time machine built by some wild eyed, crazy haired, mad scientist.

It turned out that the former members of GNR (Slash, Duff and Matt Sorum) and lead singer of STP (Scott Weiland) had just created a Supergroup to be known as Velvet Revolver.

VR's debut album *Contraband* was released during the summer of 2004, which of course I bought the day it came out. I enjoyed the album. The music sounded like Gun-n-Roses with Scott Weiland on vocals, which I was cool with. I liked the Gunner's sound and I enjoyed Weiland's vocals, so it was a match made in Rock-n-Roll heaven. Accompanying the new album was a tour, which included a Buffalo date!

As soon as tickets went on sale for the Buffalo show, I bought a pair. A month or two after tickets went on sale, the Buffalo show was canceled!

A month or so later, Velvet Revolver announced a Rochester tour date. Yet again I bought tickets and yet again the show was canceled!

I had tried twice unsuccessfully to bring my new girlfriend Shannon to a rock concert.

Fast forward a few months later to April 17, 2005. It was my 21st birthday. Shannon and I had been dating for roughly 7 months. For my birthday, Shannon surprised me with Velvet Revolver tickets! I was quite excited! The show was on Friday May 20, 2005 at PNC Bank Arts Center in Holmden, NJ. I noticed that the show was in New Jersey and I said, "Whoa! The show's in New Jersey!"

Shannon said, "Yeah, it's about a half hour or 45 minutes away from my Nana's house in Jersey."

I said, "Oh, ok."

Shannon said, "Yeah, the school semester will be done by then and I figured that we could go down for the show and you could meet the rest of my family."

I said, "Oh, ok." But secretly I was thinking, "Uh-oh! This trip is going to be the deal breaker! Apparently she likes me enough to meet the rest of her family. Hopefully they aren't weird or crazy;

otherwise I'll pull an Iron Maiden and *run to the hills, run for my life!"*

I was still living in Buffalo and Shannon was living in Rochester. Shannon wanted to leave for New Jersey early in the morning of Thursday May 19th so we could beat the NJ Parkway afternoon traffic.

That Thursday I woke up at 9am, which for me, was waking up early! After I showered and packed, I was in my car, en route to Rochester to meet up with Shannon.

Shannon was a little upset with me when I finally arrived because I was late. As far as I knew, I was on time!

We were finally on the road by late morning and eventually arrived at Nana's house in Bayville, NJ late afternoon. It was the first time I met Shannon's Nana and she seemed nice. Later that evening Shannon's Aunt Carol and Uncle Steve came over with their kids Jayson, Katie, and Tyler. They were all nice and friendly. In fact, Uncle Steve moonlighted at the PNC Arts Center as a cameraman!

The next morning Nana, Shannon, and I had bagels for breakfast. We ran around and did some errands and helped Nana out.

It was about 5pm when Shannon and I got on the NJ Parkway to head up to the PNC Arts Center.

Shannon got lawn seats, which I was totally happy with. My thought was, "As long as I'm at the venue and I can see and hear, I'm happy."

Hoobastank was the opener and they played their big songs, such as *Out Of Control, Running Away, Crawling In The Dark, Remember Me,* and *The Reason.* They also played some other songs, but I didn't know their names. Hoobastank was a good live band.

Once Hoobastank finished, Shannon and I waited about an hour for Velvet Revolver to take the stage.

A loud siren noise rang through the Arts Center and soon Velvet Revolver came out on stage and the fans cheered. With a megaphone in his one hand and the microphone in the other, lead singer Scott Weiland began singing the vocals to *Sucker Train Blues.* Weiland took to center stage on top of a speaker and sang into the megaphone during parts of the song.

Velvet Revolver continued their set with their new material off the debut album *Contraband* with *Do it for the Kids,* and *Big*

Machine. They spiced things up by playing Stone Temple Pilots' song *Crackerman.*

Weiland was dressed up in skin tight leather, donned with a German military style hat; he looked like a dominatrix. After each song, Weiland lost an article of clothing until he was just wearing the black skin tight pants and black boots.

VR also played *Spectacle, Headspace, Superhuman, Illegal I Song,* and *Dirty Little Thing.* VR slowed things down with one of their hit singles, *Fall to Pieces.*

During VR's songs, Weiland pranced around the stage while he straddled the microphone stand, he looked like a coked up pole dancer. At one point, he was leaping and bounding from speaker to speaker, to and fro, across the stage.

Weiland and Co. kicked things old school when they played Guns-n-Roses tune *It's So Easy.* Fans were delighted to hear some Gunners music.

In between songs, he asked the crowd if they wanted to hear a song from a small little band known as Stone Temple Pilots. Of course the fans roared and cheered. Weiland then started to sing, "I am, I am, I am, I said I wanna get next to you! I said I'm going to get close to you…" Fans clapped and cheered because it was the opening verse to STP's *Sex Type Thing.* During *Sex Type Thing* a fan threw a water bottle on stage and it hit Weiland square in the dome! That pissed Weiland off to the point where he stopped the song and tried to call out the ass hole that hit him. Security followed Weiland as he hopped off stage and went into the crowd to personally find the party pooper. Needless to say, Weiland never found the guy with the accurate arm. The entire time, I was a little nervous that Weiland would throw a temper tantrum, walk off stage, and end the show! Thankfully Weiland dropped the whole thing, got his scrawny junkie ass back up on stage, and finished singing *Sex Type Thing.*

Other new songs the band played were *Set Me Free* and *You Got No Right.*

VR slowed things down with a Pink Floyd cover. Lead guitarist Slash and Weiland both sat on stools in the middle of the stage. With an acoustic guitar and wearing his trademark black top hat, Slash began to strum out the opening notes to *Wish You Were Here.*

Towards the end of their set, Velvet Revolver played another Guns-n-Roses tune, *Mr. Brownstone*. Some purists may think this next statement is blasphemy, but I liked Wieland's vocals better than Axel Rose's for that song.

VR capped off a great show with their first single, *Slither*. Velvet Revolver played every song off their new album except for *Loving the Alien*.

After the show, Shannon and I hopped back into her Chevy Lumina and drove back down to Nana's house.

The following day, Shannon's family and I went out to lunch at the Sawmill. The Sawmill was located on the boardwalk in Seaside Heights and served a massive 30 inch pie! After lunch with the family, Shannon and I made the drive back home to Western New York.

PJs

(Abridged version, *The Pearl Jam Excursion,* originally appeared in Daemen College's *The Ascent,* October 21, 2005)

Grunge is basically dead. Nirvana is dead. Alice is Chains is dead (sort of, they have a new lead singer that sounds just like Layne Stanley). Soundgarden has broken up and will pretty much never get back together. But wait-don't zip up that body bag quite yet, homeslice! I still hear a faint pulse from the grunge scene, because there is still one band that is very much *Alive* and rocking out, Pearl Jam.

This leads us to September 13th, 2005, 7:30pm. The Kid (my younger sister) and I arrived at the Copps Coliseum in Hamilton, Ontario, Canada, to see Pearl Jam.

Before we ventured into the arena, we had to get some grub. We decided on Mickey D's for a couple of reasons. First of all, the MSG in all their food drew us to it. Secondly, I heard that only McDonalds in Canada still sell the McPizzas (we found that that was untrue at the three McDonalds we went to). And Lastly, we had to see if they sold quarter pounders with cheese because they use the metric system up there. The movie *Pulp Fiction* planted that seed in my head and the three McDonalds that we went to sold quarter pounders, not Royals with cheese.

While we waited at the gates, security guards patted us down. When it was my turn to be molested, I asked the security guard if I needed to turn to the left and cough. He said, "No." The guard frisked me around my waist, and I gave out a like "woo-hoo!" Then he finally let me through. The Kid was laughing hysterically.

This Pearl Jam tour was strictly a Canadian tour, hitting all of Canada's fifteen cities. Like almost every typical rock concert, there was some no-name opening act. Sleater-Kinney was the opener and the Kid and I had never heard of them. Apparently they were some chick rock band from Washington. While Sleater-Kinney played, the Kid and I wandered around and bought a couple of tour t-shirts and a poster. I also got a couple drafts of Canadian beer!

Then the lights went out and the fans began to cheer and scream. A blue light poured over the empty stage (it is rather ironic that a Blue Light was used in Canada). The PJs took the stage and the 4,500-plus fans went wild. The lights shifted from blue to a bliss of flashing red and green.

I'm not going to lie, I'm a die-hard Nirvana fan and I know all their songs inside and out. But I'm not too up to snuff with the Pearl Jam discography. Plus, Nirvana is a way far better band from Seattle than Pearl Jam could ever be. The Kid, on the other hand, is a bit of a PJs buff, so during the show, I kept on leaning over and asking her if she had heard the songs before. The Kid knew most of the songs. I can tell you that the show kicked some serious ass.

The only complaint that I had was the lack of a mosh pit on the Floor Level. There were seats everywhere, so sadly there was no room or opportunity for moshers. Another downer was that the giant jumbotron in the arena was not used. My final grievance concerned the absence of fire or pyrotechnics. It may be the inner child inside of me, but fire is really awesome!

During the show, front man Eddie Vedder really did not complain about America, except for one thing. He said simply that he loves Canada and that he wishes America could be more like it. All the Canucks were obviously cheering greatly. I turned to the Kid and said, "Do you know what he's talking about? He's got to be talking about the beer! Come on, honestly, American Beer tastes like poop!" The Kid told me that she didn't think that was what Eddie was referring to.

The PJs played a lot of old stuff, which is pretty much why anyone goes to see an old band. One of their opening songs was *Rearviewmirror*. Before they began playing this song, Eddie took out a mirror and reflected light off of it around the whole arena. They also played *Daughter*, one of their most popular songs.

The lights blackened during the show. After some darkness, a blue and purple spot-light shone upon Eddie, who placed himself center-stage with an acoustic guitar. As he began plucking out the first chords of *Jeremy*, the place turned into romper room. Suddenly, the light show kicked in and picked up when the rest of the band sounded in.

Eddie interacted with the crowd and chit-chatted a bit. He talked about the importance of keeping in touch with your very close friends, because good friends are "few and far between." After that was said, Eddie told the whole crowd that he was missing his best friend's wedding back in Seattle and placed all the blame on us. He made us all shout out, "Congratulations, Newlyweds!" to the couple of Jen and Jack. He then made us shout, "Eddie is an ass hole" to them. After that little momentary distraction, Eddie continued on with the rest of the show.

There were countless times between songs where Eddie randomly proposed a toast to all. One time in particular, he proposed a toast to Hamilton because of their donuts and coffee (yeah Tim Hortons!).

The PJs played two encores, which lasted just as long as their first set! Some of the songs they played were *Alive, Corduroy, Black, Spin the Black Circle, I Am Mine, Go, Better Man* (acoustic), *Given to Fly, Elderly Woman Behind the Counter in a Small Town* (the longest title in the Pearl Jam song catalog), *MFC, Untitled, Animal,* and many others.

During Pearl Jam's set, Sleater-Kinney came back out and helped out with a couple songs.

For the PJ's second to last song, the house lights were put on and they played a cover of Neil Young's *Keep On Rocking (In The Free World)*. They closed with *Yellow Ledbetter*.

In all, they played for close to three hours…money well spent. Sadly they did not play *Even Flow* or *Glorified G*.

Once the show ended, I still had a fist full of "funny money," four loonies to be exact. I was determined not to come back to the States with them. I quickly found one of the merchandise tables and dumped the coinage down onto the table and announced, "I need eight bumper stickers! I don't care which ones. I just need eight of them." After that, the Kid and I exited Copps Coliseum. Once we were outside, we looked around before looking at each other and I said, "Uh-no! I dunno where we parked." Luckily the Kid remembered.

It was about 1:30am when the DeLorean landed back in Buffalo. As the doors to the DeLorean opened, I looked over at the Kid, and then we both realized it was 2005 and not 1993. We both said, "Ah, crap!"

The Great Foo Fighters Outing

(Abridged version, *The Great Foo Fighters Outing*, originally appeared in Daemen College's *The Ascent*, November 22, 2005)

"It's one hundred and six miles to Chicago; we've got a tank full of gas, half a pack of cigarettes, it's dark, and we're wearing sunglasses…" Those are the famous words from Elwood Blues to his brother Jake Blues from the film *The Blues Brothers*. That was pretty much what the Kid (my little sister) and I were saying on October 3, 2005. It was around ten o'clock am when the Kid and I hopped into her Jeep to drive from South Central Grand Island to Buffalo to pick up my buddy Tony before we forged onward to Chicago for a Weezer/Foo Fighters show.

Let me give you a little background information to my story. Sometime that past August, I was surfing the net with the Kid. At the time, I was a little bummed out because I had missed the Foo Fighters show in Toronto at the Molson Amphitheater, because on the same day in Buffalo at the HSBC Arena, Green Day was playing. Since I had bought the Green Day tickets the moment they went on sale back in the spring, I was kind of bound to that show. So, sadly, I missed the Foos in Canada.

However, I soon found myself on the Foo Fighters webpage, and noticed that they were still on tour and that there were still tickets on sale for many venues. Besides hanging out with the Kid that night, I was also hanging out with Mr. Jose Cuervo and Mr. John Labatt. It was a good mix. Between the four of us, we decided that it would be wonderful to finally see the Foo Fighters.

The Kid and I love the Foo Fighters and we figured that this would be the closest that we would ever get to seeing my first love, Nirvana! I ended up buying tickets for the show in Chicago.

At first, Chicago does not look that far away from Buffalo on a map. In fact, it's only about two inches, which is no big deal. I was definitely down with it, the Kid was down, and so was my girlfriend Shannon. It was a done deal to see the Foo Fighters in Chicago.

"That's the stupidest thing you two have ever done!" Or so said the voice of reasoning coming from our mom. Mom thought it was dumb that we were hiking out to Chicago for a concert. She also thought it was the dumbest thing the Kid and I have ever done together; obviously mom doesn't know a lot.

Once school started that fall, there was a sad turn of events and Shannon was unable to make the show with the Kid and me because of stupid school. I hate how stupid school is always getting in the way of fun! Apparently Shannon had an anatomy lab practical and a quiz in clinical lab.

The show was on Monday, so the night before, the Kid and I were calling everyone we knew to see if they wanted to go to Chicago with us. Between the two of us, we called at least twenty people and we heard the same stupid sob story from everyone."Oh I'd love to go but…" I eventually called my buddy Tony from work and asked him if he wanted to go.

The following is a transcript of our conversation, derived completely from memory of course…

"Hey Tony, it's DeRose!"

"What's up dude?"

"Nothing. Do you want to go to the Weezer/Foo Fighters show tomorrow?"

"Um…what time does it start?"

"Seven thirty p.m."

"Um…well, I dunno, I have school."

"It's in Chicago!"

"Oh! Um, well, Okay!"

We picked Tony up at around 10:30am or so. We had our MapQuest directions and we headed out to the Peace Bridge. The customs officer at the station we pulled up to was scary and a tough looking mofo. He asked us where we were going and why, so we told him Chicago to see the Foo Fighters show. I guess the officer did not believe us because he asked us for our tickets. Once we showed him the tickets, we were on our way.

Crossing through Canada to get to Chicago was much faster than taking Interstate 90 from New York, through Pennsylvania, through Ohio, through Indiana, to Illinois. When we were cruising through the great country of Canada, I soon discovered that the Kid's Jeep ran out of numbers on the speedometer. We were going one hundred plus miles per hour with a tachometer that only read 3 grand, translation, we could have gone faster, but didn't. That jeep definitely had some balls.

Eventually we made it to Port Huron, Michigan, which is north of Detroit. As we traveled through Michigan, we passed by the outskirts of Detroit, through the capital Lansing, the edge of Kalamazoo, and Battle Creek, which is the home of Kellogg's!

MapQuest said it would take nine hours and change to get to the show. We made it in eight. When we arrived in Chicago, we found ourselves in the thick of rush hour traffic. We eventually found the Allstate Arena that the concert was being held at. The Allstate Arena was located right by the O'Hare Airport and right next to a strip plaza that had a Target store and Subway. Since the show started at seven thirty and it was six thirty, I thought we only had an hour to kill before the show. Then Tony informed me that I was still on Buffalo time and not Chicago time. I hadn't considered the time zone difference. So, we ended up eating breakfast at Subway and bought a twenty four pack of Bud Light. We started tailgating in the Target parking lot. Don't worry, Mr. Cuervo came along with me on the trip. He was stored safely in a Gatorade bottle.

Finally the doors opened and we made our way to the gates. I took a couple draughts of Cuervo and before I shoved Jose down my pants behind my belt. Soon enough our tickets were scanned and then we were frisked. The security guard patted my sides and then lifted up my Nirvana hoodie, and saw my Gatorade bottle. I looked down there and said, "How the hell did that get down there?!?" The guard yanked the bottle out from my pants and threw it away before he let me in. As I saw my tequila fly from the hands of the security guard to the garbage can, all I could think of was, "NOOO! That's real alcohol abuse!"

The Kaiser Chiefs were the openers and they sucked! They were thanking the crowd and crap like that…Probably thanking us for the crap that we had to put up with. They said they were from England and I shouted back from my seat at the opposite side of the arena in the two hundred level, "Go back to England! You guys suck! We want the Foo Fighters!" The Kid and Tony laughed hysterically and then denied knowing who I was.

Finally Weezer took the stage. They put on an awesome set and they didn't miss a note. They played all of their good shit with some extra goodies snuck in there too. They played *Beverly Hills, We Are All On Drugs, Buddy Holly, Undone-Sweater Song, Say it Ain't So,* and *Hash Pipe*. Weezer also covered Blur's *Song Two* (the Woo-who! Song) and the Foo Fighters' *Big Me.*

The show suffered because of an absence of pyrotechnics. Also, I saw signs that read anybody caught crowd surfing would be thrown out. Other than that, it was badass!

And then the house lights were out and the fans started screaming. The Foos took the stage and the first riffs of their song *In Your Honor* began to ring through.

The Foo Fighters could and should have played for hours. The Kid said they played for about two hours. Considering they have five albums out (one being a double disc), they could have play forever. The Foos played a lot of new stuff from their latest double disc release, which they were on tour promoting, *In Your Honor*, but they also included a lot of songs from their previous albums. Such songs they ripped out were *All My Life, My Hero, Best of You, Learn To Fly, Up In Arms, Times Like These, Last Song, The One, Stacked Actors, DOA, This Is A Call, End Over End, Breakout,* and *Everlong*. While *Everlong* was playing, I looked over to the Kid and said, "Crap, this is it. This song is known for being their closer."

Fortunately for all of us, the Foos proved me wrong. The Foo Fighters' drummer Taylor Hawkings walked away from his drum kit to front center stage. Hawkings picked up an acoustic guitar while front man and lead singer Dave Grohl took his seat at the drums. Hawkings said he was going to sing a new song, *Cold Day In The Sun*. The Foos ended up closing the show with one of their best and most kick ass songs, *Monkeywrench*.

After we left the show, the Kid drove because Tony and I were not in any shape to be driving. So the first hour and a half of our trip home consisted of us just sitting in the Target parking lot because of the huge traffic jam of concert attendees going home.

After we got on the road, Tony and I made the Kid pull over because the two of us had to piss like race horses. The Kid ended up pulling over on the side of the road next to a funeral home. But don't worry, it's not what you think, Tony and I did not piss on the funeral home, just the front bushes. As Tony and I were going, Tony looked over his shoulder and said, "Holy shit dude! A cop's coming! Get back in the truck!" So I had to pinch myself off, midstream, to get back before the cop came. Once in the Jeep, the Kid asked what the problem was and we informed her that a cop had just pulled up behind her. Of all people, the Kid asked two drunken idiots what to do. Tony quickly chimed in and told her to not pull away, but to stay put. The cop sat behind us for a good five minutes before he pulled up alongside of us and said, "Everything okay? Good. Okay. Bye." And that was that.

The Kid eventually got us lost. We ended up pulling over in a parking lot of a tiny plaza at five thirty am. We slept in the Jeep until eight or nine in the following morning. Once we woke, we were soon on the road. We eventually pulled into a gas station because we needed gas and we were totally lost. As I walked into the store, still drunk or buzzed, I approached the cashier with a map at hand.

"Hello, how can I help you," inquired the cashier.

"Hi, I'm lost," I replied.

"Well, where are you headed?"

"Buffalo."

"Buffalo?"

"Yea, Buffalo."

"Buffalo?"

"Yea, Buffalo…New York…You know, the Bills, four time in a row Super Bowl losers…Buffalo."

"Oh…*Buffalo!* Man, you're a long ways away from home."

"I know…"

The cashier ended up giving me directions for us to get back onto the main drag to catch the highway we needed.

Long story short, the Kid drove around aimlessly after the show until the wee hours of the morning and got us nowhere. I think we were still in Indiana, just outside Michigan. So that meant the Kid drove around for four or five hours and got us nowhere as opposed to half way home already.

Once we were back in Canada, I made a point of having the Kid make a small detour while we were driving through London, Ontario. My motive; I wanted to see the Labatt Brewery. The Kid was a little pissed off. She said, "This is worse than taking an alcoholic to a bar. Now I'm just taking one to the headquarters of the problem." What can I say? I had to see the brewery! It was like a pilgrimage for me. My trip to the Labatt Brewery is tantamount to a Christian going to Jerusalem or a Muslim going to Mecca. So we saw the brewery, but we did not take the tour because we did not have the time.

We finally arrived back in Buffalo on Tuesday, October 4th. The Kid and I looked at the concert shirts we had purchased while there, and one of them listed all the cities the tour was hitting. The Foos were also playing in Detroit and Cleveland. "Man! Adam! How drunk were you when you bought those tickets?!"

I chuckled and said, "Do you think we can out do ourselves and hit up the show in Cleveland?"

NIN

Back in the end of January 2006, I was at work and I asked my boss Mr. Morgan of PS Cleaning Service if I could have March 9th off. He asked me why I needed that date off and I told him that I wanted the night off for the Nine Inch Nails show. Rightfully so, Mr. Morgan, knowing my track record with rock concerts, asked "What state?"

I was puzzled and asked, "What?"

Mr. Morgan replied with, "What country? What time zone?"

By this time, I knew that he was having fun with me. I said, "Oh you don't need to worry Mr. Morgan, the show is not in Canada, Chicago, or New Jersey."

Mr. Morgan said, "Oh, really Adam. Then where is the concert?"

I said, "No need to worry Mr. Morgan. It's in Rochester."

Mr. Morgan quickly chimed back with, "Which Rochester?! There's a couple Rochesters out there!"

I told Mr. Morgan that the gig was at the Blue Cross Arena in Rochester, NY.

After getting the night off, I bought three tickets for the show. It was a definite that I was going and so was my home boy Brian. I bought a third ticket. I asked my girlfriend Shannon to go, but yet again like clockwork, her stupid school classes got in the way. I really needed to talk to her teachers and tell them to quit having tests and classes on the days of kick ass rock concerts. I asked my sister to go, but she had class too. My buddy "Trans Am" Mike had night classes and my other buddy Jason really didn't feel like going. Thankfully the ticket did not end up going to waste though. Jay, one of the dudes Brian worked with at Cameo's Restaurant said he would go.

It was finally March 9th. Brian and I went to Cameo's Restaurant, on Niagara Falls Boulevard, around 4:30pm because we had to wait for Jay to get off work. Once Jay's shift ended, we pregamed at the bar there…a couple beers and shots. Once we had Jay and a few beers and shots in our systems, we hit the road.

We were on the road by 5:15pm and were making good time. We took the 90 eastbound to I-490. Once we were on 490, we were all pretty hungry and I had to piss like a race horse, so we stopped off on Exit 4, Chili. We wanted pizza and we weren't going to eat that Pizza Hut crap so we found a dinky little pizza joint called Phil's Pizza. It must have been the only place in town without a bathroom, but we made our own on the outside of the building. We had about 15 minutes to kill so we wandered for a bit. While we wandered, I had some Jose Cuervo with me that I subsequently spilled it all over myself as I drank it. I had to change because I was a little wet and just wreaked of tequila (a good rule of thumb—use the buddy system and NEVER leave home without Jose).

The three of us stumbled upon a plaza that had a Bill Gray's restaurant. Brian could not wait the 15 minutes for our pizza, so he ordered a couple white hot dogs and downed them like they were nothing.

15 minutes came and went and we had our pie and we were back on the road.

Before long, we were in downtown Rochester. I've never been to the Blue Cross Arena, but I've seen it from the highway numerous times. Brian's been to the BCA but didn't really remember how to get there. So there we were, like three chickens with our heads chopped off, driving around lost in downtown Rochester. We ended up driving past the Genesee Brewery. We drove around in a couple more circles and Brian ended up rolling down his window to ask some pedestrians where the BCA was. They looked at us and pointed right in front of us. Duh!

We found a parking spot that gave us rock star parking…it was right by the exit to the highway.

Once inside the lobby of the BCA, we did a little people watching. The crowd that we saw in line really didn't look like the folks that you would see at a Nine Inch Nails show. There were some kids and older folks, but definitely no people decked out in all black with makeup on. Not a freak to be seen anywhere!

We soon found our seats. We were on the 200 level, right next to the stage.

To say the least, the opening act was not my favorite. Sean Williams may have been a hit with some people, but he did not click or connect with me. I'm not discounting his talent, but he wasn't for me. Williams' music was a cross between rap and hard rock. His style was different. The band consisted of Williams and some dude on a turn table behind him. The dude on the turn table was actually extremely good and spun out some good funky and hard sounding shit. Williams on the other hand looked a bit out of place...I had not seen too many brothers with a Mohawk. Almost all of William's material was politically based. Hey, I'm going to a rock concert to hear rock-n-roll, not politics. If I want to hear stuff about politics, I'll hang out with my grandparents and watch C-SPAN or I'll actually pay attention and listen to the crap that my college professors were preaching about in class. Anyway, Williams was just talking into the mic a mile per minute. If he rapped, that would be cool, but he wasn't doing that. Thankfully he only played for a half hour.

Finally NIN took the stage. There was a curtain around the entire stage with white spot lights that made silhouettes of everything on stage. For the entire first song, the curtain was up. It wasn't until the beginning of the second song when the curtain was dropped. Their third song they played was *Terrible Lie,* during which there was a spectacle of strobe lights and neons flashing everywhere.

NIN also played *Piggy*. During *Piggy*, founder and front man Trent Reznor disarmed himself of his axe and hopped off the stage and started walking around in front of the pit, high fiving fans.

During *March Of The Pigs*, one of the guitarists, still playing his guitar, ran and jumped off the stage into the crowd where he crowd surfed!

It was a little weird seeing Trent Reznor with a shaved head and some extra muscle. Looking like that, he kind of reminded me of Henry Rollins. Well, I guess I was just so used to seeing him as a skinny dude with black hair covering his eyes...oh well.

On the floor, there was a huge crowd of people but they weren't rocking out or anything. All the fans just stood there. There were about a handful of crowd surfers, but that was it. Fans tried to start a mosh pit about three times, but it had a half-life of 30 seconds.

People watching was fun; two rows in front of us was a zombie like girl. Sure when bands first come out on stage and for the next couple songs, people stand, but eventually they sit down. No. Not this girl. For the whole two hour long show, she stood. The one guy sitting behind her was getting frustrated because he couldn't see.

Another dude in the row in front of us was just going ape shit crazy. I had no idea how to justly explain what he was doing, but he was just a wild man. He had his head shaven and was just sweating profusely.

Behind us and over a section, two dudes were going insane on air drums.

A few rows back, three dudes were having their own mini mosh pit in the seats. There were definitely more weirdoes at the show, but there's not enough time to describe the others.

Some other songs Nine Inch Nails cranked out were *Burn, Eraser, Gave Up, Head Like A Hole, Suck, The Frail, The Wretched, The Great Below, The Mark Has Been Made, Wish,* and *The Day The World Went Away*. I can't really remember the other songs they played because they played for two hours. Buzzed or sober, it is still pretty damn hard to remember two hours' worth of songs.

During NIN's set, the curtain was raised above the stage and a movie was projected onto the curtain. The whole concept was pretty cool. The film quality and direction resembled that of an independent film. After a couple songs, the curtain was dropped again.

The pit began to show signs of life when NIN started to play the beginning notes of *Closer*. For this song, the entire stage was illuminated only by red lights, which gave a sense of feel towards the Red Light District, which fit in perfectly with the lyrics of *Closer…you let me violate you…you let me penetrate you…I want to fuck you like an animal…I want to feel you from the inside…*

After the meat and potatoes of the show, Nine Inch Nails played some of their new songs, *With Teeth, Only,* and *Every day Is Exactly The Same*. During *Every Day*, there was a huge wide screen movie screen that spanned the entire length of the back of the stage. On it, they showed huge desert sand dunes and it progressed from there. I think NIN ended up closing the show with *Hurt*. And one of the really cool things they did at the end of the show that ruled was they destroyed the guitars!! YES! YES! Destroy! Destruction!

After Brian, Jay, and I arrived back in Buffalo, we stopped off at Vizzy's on Kenmore Ave. and topped off the night with a couple night caps.

The following day I told Shannon all about the concert. She seemed very bummed out that she was unable to go to the show.

A few months later NIN was playing up north of the border at the Molson Amphitheater of Saturday June 24th. I took Shannon and she absolutely loved the show!

While at the concert Shannon and I won tickets for Edgefest 2006, which was at the Molson Amphitheater the following weekend.

The following weekend Shannon and I were back up in T.O. for another concert. Edgefest 2006 was the 20th anniversary for the Canadian based rock concert series. Shannon and I got to see Keane, Hot Hot Heat, and Our Lady Peace.

Shannon was a little bummed out because she thought we won tickets to Edgefest Two, which was a later that month. Edgefest Two had Yellowcard and the All-American Rejects headlining. Needless to say we couldn't get our paws on tix to that show.

Foo Fighting Again

I was wandering around on the internet again and saw that the Foo Fighters were playing in Atlantic City. I called up my girlfriend Shannon and asked her if she wanted to visit her family in New Jersey in August. She said, "Yea, of course!" Then I asked her if she wanted to see the Foo Fighters in Atlantic City and she of course said, "Yea!" again, considering she missed them last fall due to stupid classes. I also knew that if I took Shannon, that she would keep me in line and not let me get plastered, like the first time I saw the Foos.

The show was on Friday August 18th 2006. The departure started at Shannon's house in Rochester. Shannon's Nana was chill-axing for a couple weeks with Shannon's parents and when we went down for the show we were going to drop Nana off at her house because she lived about one hour away from Atlantic City. We probably left Rachacha at around 8am.

The drive to Atlantic City, on a good day, should have taken us about 8ish hours. We were making great time through NY and PA. Even when we hit NJ we were ahead of schedule. Then we hit the NJ Parkway. Once we hit the traffic on the parkway, it was about 3pm and we were only about 40 miles away from Nana's house…it took almost an hour and a half to get to Nana's. Shannon and I were freaking out a little bit because we thought the show started at 7pm and we didn't know if there was going to be an opener. Plus, on top of that, we had to deal with the bumper to bumper traffic from Nana's house in Toms River down to Atlantic City. We finally arrived at Nana's a little before 5pm. Shannon and I showered and then took off.

Once Shannon and I hopped back into the car, I looked at the tickets and realized that I'm still a Pollock…the show did not start until 8pm…we had an extra hour. We managed to hop back onto the Parkway and headed towards Atlantic City.

As we neared exits for the A.C., I had no real idea where I was going because I have never been to Atlantic City. I saw the sign that said Atlantic City Express Way, so I hopped on it. Soon we saw a sign that said Philly 52 miles and soon after another sign that said Philly 42. That's when I said, "Shit, I think we're going the wrong way." We soon came upon toll booths and I asked the booth lady where Atlantic City was and she pointed behind me. I said, "Ok, thank you, I'm a dumb ass." So we pulled a U-dog and headed the correct way. We finally made it to A.C. a little before 7. We found the Borgata Casino without any problems. Yes, the show was at a casino. I found it a little weird too considering I've never been to a rock concert at a casino.

Shannon and I did not want to do valet parking because we wanted to "pregame" a little before the show. We found some normal parking on the casino grounds. We popped open the tail gate and started kicking back some Johnny Bootleggers that I found for $1.99 a bottle at the Raintree Convenient store in Tonawanda. Those things were awesome! They came in little 8 oz. bottles and had 12% alcohol. I got the green flavor because that's all they had, and they tasted exactly like a sour apple jolly rancher…I highly recommend them; they definitely give you the most bang for your two bucks.

After we polished off the Johnnies, we ventured into the casino. I remembered that at the casinos in Vegas, the waitress will serve you free drinks if you were playing the games. A soon as we walked in, I was dead set on getting my free Coronas! Shannon said she had to go to the bathroom and I told her ok and that I would get us some Coronas from the cocktail waitress because I saw one in front of us. Shannon said, "NO! Absolutely not!" She apparently thought that I was checking out the waitress from head to heels. The cocktail waitress was wearing nothing but high heels, long stockings, super short skirt (where if she bent down, well…you know) and a tight little top with her…well you get the picture. So I escorted Shannon to the bathroom.

Let me tell you, I liked going to the bathrooms at casinos because they were always so clean and fancy looking! They had a "bathroom jockey" in there to dry your hands I guess if you wanted to. *Thanks, but no thanks; I can dry my own hands.*

Since we were at that casino Shannon and I needed to find out where the show was. There was a theater and I asked the casino employee there if that was where that concert was. He asked which show. I said, "The Foo Fighters! Who else?" He said that Chris Isaac was playing at the doors we were at and that we needed to go to the other end of the casino, so we did.

Once we got to the ballroom where the Foos were playing, we discovered that there was an opener. To kill some time, Shannon and I bought concert t-shirts. We dropped them back off at the car because we did not want to hold onto them throughout the whole show. We did not care for the opener, not that I even remembered their name.

On tap at the venue was the worst beer selection: Heineken and Amstel Light. But I thought, "Beer is beer...beggars can't be choosers." Once we had beer, we went in to see the opener.

The opener finally closed their set with a cover of an AC/DC song.

Intermission: Pee breaks and reloads on poop tasting beer. Then back to make our way back to the stage because we had floor tickets. Since the venue had not filled up, Shannon and I were able to stand front and center of the stage!

The folks that showed up to see the Foos really surprised me considering that there were not a whole hell of a lot of kids. The majority of the crowd was 30 and 40 something, though Shannon and I were in our early 20s.

Kill the lights...Screams...Enter Foos. The Foos kicked off the night with *Everlong*, which was extremely odd because *Everlong* is known for being their "closer."

The Foo Fighters followed *Everlong* with *My Hero* and *Low*.

During *Monkey Wrench*, the band started screwing around and playing random riffs and their own thing and got away from the song at the really cool part where Dave yells/screams at the very end...but don't worry, they got back to the end of the song and everyone was singing the refrain along with the song.

After a few songs, founder/lead vocalist/guitarist Dave Grohl said that he was going to try to keep the chit chat at a minimum because there was not enough time to talk and figured that we all wanted to hear music as opposed to talk.

The Foos continued to play other songs such as *Best of You, DOA, Times Like These, Hey, Johnny Park!,* and *Learn to Fly.*

During *Stacked Actors*, Dave Grohl hopped off stage and walked over to where the grand stand seats and floor section met. He then proceeded to go right into the stands and started ripping out flaying guitar riffs. Back on stage, guitarist Chris Shiflett countered with his solo arsenal of riffs and strums. The two went back and forth for about five minutes before Dave got back onto the stage and finished *Stacked Actors.*

At one point during the show in between songs, Dave said that they have never played in Atlantic City and felt that only the weirdest of the weird would have come out to Atlantic City of all places to hear them…P.S. the show was sold out. Dave also went on to say that there were two things in life that you should never do, "crack and gambling." He said how he worked too hard for his money to piss it away at a casino. He continued on that thought and said that he did not like to gamble at all, but a couple years ago he did make a gamble. He said that it was a gamble that paid off greatly and that gamble was bringing drummer Taylor Hawkins on board. After saying that, Dave turned away from the audience and made his way towards the front of Taylor's drum kit and said how he had a love song to sing to him. That's when Dave started to sing the beginning of *Up In Arms Again.*

The house lights went out…time for the encore! Woo-hoo! The Foos kicked off the encore with *Aurora.* They followed *Aurora* up with *A Cold Day in the Sun.* During that song, the drummer Taylor hopped out from his drum kit to take center stage. A roadie handed him a guitar and Dave took his place at the drums. The last song the Foos played was *Breakout.* Then the show was over. The roadies were throwing drum sticks and picks out into the crowd…Shannon managed to get a guitar pick.

The only crummy part of the show was that the Foos did not play their cover of Prince's *Darling Nikki* nor did they play *The One* or play anything off their first record *Foo Fighters.*

After we exited the ballroom, we waited around for a bit in the lobby until it cleared out. As we were walking away from the crowd, some drunken ass hole with his wasted *friend* (she probably was an escort) was yelling at Shannon because the stupid girl fell into Shannon. The douche bag yelled to Shannon to watch where she was walking. Before I knew what had happened, dumb and dumber walked away. Lucky for them because I was ready to kick some ass! Or so I would like to have thought.

Shannon always said that no matter where we went, I always saw some dude from Buffalo. So it was no surprise that when I saw some dude wearing a backwards Bills hat, I asked him, "Hey dude, you from Buffalo?"

"Yea dude, from Sanborn. You?"

Shannon just shook her head.

I said, "South Central Grand Island."

Shannon shook her head again.

After the lobby cleared, it was time to gamble! I was not a big gambler, let alone a high roller; I just loved the free drinks that the half-naked waitresses serve me! But my friends, it is time to go. Unfortunately right now is not the time and/or place to hear the casino part of the story. Until we meet again, party on!

Family Values

Ladies and gents, it is now time for some Family Values…

The Family Values tour hit Darien Lake Performing Arts Center on August 29, 2006. And like most concerts, where you normally get your tickets a head of time, such was the case for my home boy Brian and me. We were chillin' in his basement earlier in the summer and I asked him, "Do you want to see Korn? They're head lining the Family Values tour."

Brian was hemming and hawing about going considering we had already seen them two years ago at Darien Lake when they were a part of the Projekt Revolution tour. I told him that lawn seats were only $10 a pop.

Then Brian said, "Why not." Brian left the ticket situation up to me and he went to go pee.

I logged onto the internet and found a ticket sales website and went through the bullshit to obtain tickets—credit card number, phone number, library card, reference from a neighbor—all that fun stuff. The final step to buy the tickets was to hit the confirm button, so I did. After that, three pop-ups took over the screen and I freaked out and closed all the windows, including the ticket confirmation window.

Just then, Brian came out from his "office" and heard me swearing up a storm. I told him what happened and he said, "No big deal."

We then went to the same website and he went through all the steps that I did. Brian got to the confirmation page and I told him that I did all that crap and after I hit the button, I got attacked with pop-ups. He hit the button and his order went through. That's it. Just then, the rust wheels in our head started to turn and the light bulbs went on. Then us two Pollocks realized we had just bought 8 tickets to Korn, as opposed to the four tickets that we initially wanted. Oh well, we knew enough people to pawn the tickets off on…or so we thought. We initially got enough people to take our remaining tickets, but like usual, when push comes to shove, nothing ever worked out.

So, fast forward a few months later to the end of August. Brian, his girlfriend Teri, and our buddy "Trans Am Mike" picked up Shannon and me at Daemen College. After we all crammed into

Teri's Chevy Malibu, it was off to the concert! The concert started at around 2 or 3 in the afternoon. All the bands, except for Korn, pretty much sucked, so we left closer to 6pm. Korn was not taking the stage until 9, so we had plenty of time to tail gate and pregame.

Once we got to the parking lot at Darien Lake, it was time to play ball! We threw a blanket over the trunk of the Chevy and busted out the cups for Beer Pong! Brian could not find ping pong balls, so he ended up buying a bag of cat toys that had some foam balls in the package.

Game 1- Bros vs. Hoes. Mike and I were playing against Teri and Shannon. Mike and I cleaned up shop in that game. The girls kept it a close game, but they were no match for Team Ramrod.

Game 2- Mike and me versus Teri and Brian. Mike and I decided to stay on the same team considering we had a winning streak going on. Game 2 started off with Teri and Brian sinking their first two shots, so they got to shoot again. Eventually it was Team Ramrod's turn. We nailed some cups, but for the most part, no one could sink any shots that game; though there were a fair share of ringers that did not drop in. Finally it was down to the wire! Brian and Teri only had 1 cup left and Team Ramrod had 2 cups. It Team Ramrod's shot. I missed on my attempt but Mike came through in the clutch and sank his shot! Brian and Teri had redemptions. Mike and I were gloating and taunting them on how they were not going to make their shots. Well, the two of them must have had a horse shoe up their ass or something because they nailed both of their shots! OVERTIME!

Sudden death overtime consisted of three cups a piece and wouldn't you know it, but overtime came down to the wire too! Both teams were down to one cup. I shot first and missed way wide. Mike was on a hot steak and nailed his cup. Since it was sudden death overtime, there were no redemptions for Brian and Teri. Team Ramrod was victorious and undefeated! 2-0!

It was getting a little dark in the parking lot and we would have continued to play a little more pong, but we couldn't see all that well. Plus we lost all the balls except for one. Instead, we just hung out and made fun of each other and people watched.

During Beer Pong, some dude wearing a Slayer jacket was stumbling around, bouncing off car to car. As he walked right through our beer pong game, he was mumbling and talking to himself. We were all pretty sure that guy did not know where he was.

Soon after, some other dude was walking briskly by our Pong game and asked us if we had any acid. We all just kind of looked at each other and said, "No," before giggling. Brian chimed in, "I think that Slayer kid ate all that kid's acid."

About a half hour later, a group of kids were walking by and one of them asked us if we had any NOS. Brian replied, "Any NOS?"

The kid said, "Yea, nitrous oxide."

I said, "Yea, we know what that is, but we don't have any. This thing's a 2002 Chevy Malibu, not a '67 dude."

Another dude got kicked out of the concert or was too drunk and didn't realize he accidentally left the show. Whatever the case was, he wanted to get back in, so Brian sold him one of our extra tickets.

The string of loonies and crazies didn't end there. Some other dude wanted a beer and Mike was trying to sell him one of my Labatts for $5. The dude wouldn't pay $5 for a beer, so Mike ended up settling on $1 for the sale of the brew. Of course Mike sold *my* beer and kept the dollar for himself. Fucker!

Soon it was time to head towards the gates because the Deftones just finished their stupid set. I speak for my whole crew when I say the Deftones suck and that is why we pregamed in the parking lot.

So we rallied the troops (the Molsons and a tiny bottle of tequila) and headed towards the venue. I'm pretty sure that Brian and Mike were double fisting, because I know that I was.

It felt like no time to walk up to the gates for the show and I still had a third beer to down on top of the tequila. Mike, Brian, and Teri hate tequila, so it was up to Shannon and me to kill the baby bottle. The two of us couldn't finish the bottle, so I popped it into my pocket, hoping that the security guard would not feel it. Shockingly the security guard did not give me a DRE (digital rectal exam). Even better was that I was able to sneak the tequila into the event! Woo-hoo!

Our tickets were lawn seats. Even though there are no seats on the lawn, we apparently had seats. Even if we wanted to sit, it was a huge muddy mess…

Lights go out…screams…

No intro, no "Hey how you doing", just loud heavy thumping and throbbing of bass, guitar, and drums. Eventually Jonathan Davis, the vocalist, said, "Hey what's up, we're here to fucking rock!" Korn then opened with *Right Now*.

Korn was touring in support of their latest album, *See You on the Other Side*. From that album, they played *Politics, Coming Undone,* and *Twisted Transistor*; though *Twisted Transistor* was saved for the encore. Additionally, we got free lithograph prints of the album cover.

Shannon wanted to try crowd surfing, so Mike and I hoisted her up. She went about…hmm…not even two feet before she was dropped on her butt. I did not have much success either.

During the set, Chino, the lead man from the Deftones, came out on the stage and rap/sang a metal duet with Jonathan from Korn, *Wicked*. It wasn't good at all.

It didn't take long for the mosh pit to start behind us and even less time for all of us to join in, except for Teri. She was kind of the "mom" for the night because she was the designated driver. Also, she held onto my glasses and bottle of tequila.

Moshing=fun!

Moshing=dirty!

Moshing=football hits and bright lights in the pitch black of night!

Korn also played fan favorites *Falling Away From Me, Got The Life, Freak On a Leash, ADIDAS, Shoots and Ladders,* and a couple others that escape me right now. They came back for an encore that included *Twisted Transistor, Y'All Want a Single,* and *Blind*.

Korn ended up playing for close to an hour and a half.

The show was cool in all, but the last time I saw Korn was so much better.

After the show, we returned to the Malibu to drink some more beer and wait for traffic to clear out. Once the traffic cleared out, we busted a move.

Zombies&gods

There was nothing like school to make you late for having fun: case in point, going to the Rob Zombie and Godsmack concert on September 4, 2006 at Darien Lake Performing Arts Center.

Shannon and I were stuck at cross country practice which did not end until after 6pm…the workout for practice was to run for 80 minutes and it sucked. To make matters worse, practice was not held on campus at Daemen College. It was held off campus, at Beaver Island State Park; translation, Shannon and I were an extra 20 minutes further away from Darien Lake.

Since we have this part established, Shannon and I still had to shower, eat, get booze, and rendezvous with my friends Mike and Brian at Brian's parent's house…plus the show started at 7pm. What did all that mean? Well it meant that we missed the opener Shinedown, who I kind of wanted to see.

Mike was a speed demon, so we rolled into our parking spot at Darien Lake by 7:30pm. After we hopped outta Mike's Durango, we tailgated for a bit because Shinedown's set had just ended and we did not want to rush right in and wait around for a half hour before the next set. Anyway, we killed a couple cans of Sparks (6.0% alcoholic energy drinks that tasted like Smarties candy) and Brian brought the left over Molsons from the Korn concert with us (the week prior, we saw Korn at the same venue). After finishing off the leftover beers, tailgating ended, and we walked up to the venue.

As we were walking through security Rob Zombie took the stage.

After getting our colonoscopies done by the security guards we made our way to our seats, which were underneath the canopy.

Let me tell you, Rob Zombie was just mind blowing; every aspect of his show was just awesome—fire and half naked chicks!

Zombie's stage performance was just spectacular! The pyrotechnics kicked ass, whether it was the little puff balls of fire or the five seconds of light torches, it was great! Along with the fire, the stage props were cool too. There were huge American flags that had skulls on them. Zombie also used the jumbotron. It was on stage and showed old cheesy horror movies like the Munsters, along with bits from his movies, and half naked chicks. And then there were the scantily clad zombie cheerleaders who were go-go dancing from cages suspended from the canopy. It was hot and a **BIG** turn on.

During Zombie's set, he performed a cover of Metallica's *Enter Sandman* which fucking rocked!

Midway through the set, Rob Zombie asked the audience if they wanted to hear anything from his old band White Zombie and the fans went crazy. Rob figured that that was a "yes" and then decided to play *Thunder Kiss '65,* and *More Human Than Human.* And yes, they even played the full length intro to *More Human Than Human* where the girl moaned as if she was cumming.

During *House of 1000 Corpses* clips from Rob Zombie's movie "House of 1000 Corpses" was being shown on the jumbotron.

When *The Devil's Rejects* was being performed, clips from Zombie's movie "The Devil's Rejects" were being shown along with the Manson gang and their mug shots.

In between songs, a video was put up on the main stage's video monitor. The theme music from the slasher flick *Halloween* could be heard over the speakers. We fans soon realized that we were watching a sneak peak teaser trailer to Rob Zombie's remake of the *Halloween* movie, due next Halloween season, October 2007.

Other songs that Rob Zombie played were *Dragula, Living Dead Girl, Never Gonna Stop (The Red Red Kroovy),* and *Feel So Numb.*

Though the set was about an hour long, Rob Zombie & Co. put on a hell of a show!

During the set change, I had to squirt and replenish my beer.

After waiting forever in a line to pee, I had to wait in another long line for beer. Finally it was my time to walk up to the concession counter and order my tall overpriced beer!

As my beer was being poured, the stage lights went out. Being played over the speakers were the sound of gun fire and helicopters! It was the intro to Godsmacks' *Straight out of Line.*

Godsmack was on tour promoting their fourth studio album, *IV*, thus playing a few new cuts to the liking of *Speak* and *The Enemy.*

Godmack did not disappoint, they played a lot of their hits and fan favorites including *Moon Baby, Realign, Awake, Trippin,* and *Keep Away.*

Shannon even got to hear her favorite Godsmack song, *Voodoo*.

I was surprised to hear Godsmack play their instrumental song *Vampires*.

Towards the end of their set, lead singer and rhythm guitarist Sully Erna and drummer Shannon Larkin played *Batalla de los Tambores*; better known as the dueling drums! Erna and Larkin each manned their own drum kit, surrounded 360° by drums, so no matter which way they spun on their chair, they could hit their notes. Each drum kit was on a moving platform that moved and rotated across and around the stage. To top it off, they even dueled with bongos!

Godsmack ended their set with *Whatever*. When they we done playing, their songs had me so amped up that I wanted to kick someone's ass because that's the kind of music they played, kick ass music!

Thankfully Godsmack came out for an encore to calm me down.

For the encore, Godsmack played new song *Shine Down* and kick ass song *I Stand Alone*. After hearing *I Stand Alone*, I wanted to kick someone's ass again, but I did not.

Once the show ended, concert goers started to file out. Shannon, Brian, Mike, and I waited a bit for the crowd to die down a little before we started our exodus.

A group of kids walked down the aisle and passed by us. The girl in the group tripped over and fell down. Everyone noticed the girl take a tumble; it was hard to miss.

Recently Mike had joined the volunteer fire department up in Wheatfield, NY, so Mike was fully ready and willing to help. Mike popped out of his seat and rushed over to see if he could be of any assistance.

Brian and I joked around that Mike needed to "secure the perimeter" around the girl and then perform "dong to mouth" resuscitation to save her life.

Mike came back moments later.

Shannon was all concerned and asked Mike, "What happened? Is she okay?"

All smug, Mike said, "Yea, she's fine. She's just another drunk."

Brian asked, "Well why didn't you save her Mike?"

You could tell that Mike was getting a little annoyed and agitated as he exasperated, "Because she was drunk! There was nothing I could do…"

I questioned Mike, "What? There was nothing you could do? She didn't need any schlong to mouth resuscitation?"

Shannon tried not to laugh as Brian cackled like a school girl.

"Fuck you guys!" Mike belted out.

Brian and I giggled like Beavis and Butt-Head for the whole walk back to the car. Mike eventually laughed about it later.

Foos Unplugged

For those who know me, they always know I'm always doing something dumb and stupid…it's common knowledge. With that being said, none of my friends or family were surprised when I bought tickets to an acoustic show of the Foo Fighters. For those of you out there saying, "Oh no, not another one of these stupid Foo Fighter story…" well, this story is different. It's different in that it was an acoustic show, not a rock show and that it was out of the country...

The show was at Scotiabank Place; home of the Ottawa Senators. I figured that I should get directions off Yahoo! Maps considering I had no real idea where I was going. So in the little map box, I typed in 'Scotiabank Place' for the address and 'Ottawa' for the city and 'Canada' for the country. The computer gave me directions and said Buffalo was only 5 hours and 15 minutes away. That sounded good to me.

Shannon and I drove up in my '94 Saturn SC2 that's rockin' 155K miles.

The show was being played Sunday, November 5th, 2006. I figured that if we left Buffalo by 10am, my girlfriend Shannon and I would have enough time to get to Ottawa. We finally left Buffalo at 1pm, right when the Buffalo Bills game started. We listened to the Green Bay Packers @ Buffalo Bills game on the radio until we lost reception.

Four hours later, Shannon and I were at the US and Canadian Border in the 1000 Islands, New York. I had no idea what it was, but every time I was at the border, I inadvertently chose the lane with the longest time wait. Finally we made it up to the customs booth. The customs officer wanted our IDs. Shannon was all fancy and had her passport. I had my driver's license. The customs officer asked me where my birth certificate was. "Huh? My what?"

The officer said, "Your birth certificate Mr. DeRose."

That dinky sheet of paper was at home in some folder stuffed in some closet where I had no idea where it was. The customs officer told me that I could not get into the country without my birth certificate. I was thinking, "Are you *freaking* kidding me!?" I told the man that I was from Buffalo and that I always went up to Canada via the Falls and that all we needed was our driver's licenses.

His response to that was that the Falls was obviously a bit more relaxed than up there in the 1000 Islands and blaa blaa blaa…Eventually he asked where we were going and I told him to Scotiabank Place in Ottawa to see the Foo Fighters open for Bob Dylan. The customs officer eventually let us into Canada…

Man, if that dude wouldn't have let us into Canada, I was not about to drive the four hours back home. There probably would have been a scene with red and blue lights and guns drawn at me, but that never happened, so I was just ducky!

Shannon and I made it into downtown Ottawa by 6:30pm. Great! We had an hour 'til the show started. All we needed to do was find Scotiabank Place, park, and then get food in our tummies because we were hungry.

So those directions I told you about, yea I fudged up on them. Yahoo! Maps did not recognize Scotiabank Place as an address, so the directions dumped us off in front of Parliament. It didn't take us long to realize we were lost, so I stopped off at a Delta Chelsea hotel for directions. The helpful Canadians gave us a map and directions. They said SBP was about a half hour away.

I hopped back into the Saturn, which was still puttering along like the Little Engine That Could.

When I got back in the car, it was 7pm! No need to worry, because by 7:18, Shannon and I were pulling into our parking spot right in front of Scotiabank Place!

Shannon and I made it to our seats in the nose bleeds right as Scotiabank Place cut out the house lights…

The Foo Fighters came out on stage, lights came on, and each band member sat in a seat by their instrument. Dave Grohl, the lead singer said something along the lines of, "Hey what's up? We're the Foo Fighters. I'll give introductions later." Then Dave started to play the first repeating cords to *Times Like These* before he told the crowd what the name of the song was.

The next song played was *Marigold*. *Marigold* was the only Nirvana song that Dave Grohl wrote and sang for the group.

I was not exactly sure what the next song they played was. Shannon and I did not pregame before the concert mainly because there was no time to. Plus it would have felt weird to get loaded before an acoustic concert. If anything, this concert had the feel of drinking Mimosas (orange juice and champagne) on a Thanksgiving

Day morning. Anyway, I think the next song they played was *Next Year*.

It was during either *See You* or *Up In Arms* where during the song, Dave stopped singing and decided to give the introductions to all his band mates…

First to be introduced was Rami Jaffee who played the piano, melodeon, organ, and the accordion. Rami had a solo on the piano.

Next in line was Pat Smear who used to play with Dave in a little band called Nirvana. Pat was playing the electric and acoustic guitars. Pat did not give solos.

Pat was followed by guitarist Chris Shiflett who had his own little mini solo where he tore it up with his ax.

Petra Haden had the next intro. In addition to backup vocals, she played the violin and mandolin. After her violin solo, Dave said that she was the "Mother fucking Jimmy Page of violins!"

Then the Foos' bassist, Nate Mendel, was introduced. Nate played his little bass solo and then Dave made fun of him. Dave said, "Yea, Nate is coming out with a solo album soon. It's gonna consist of 43 minutes of him playing the same four notes, some in different keys…kinda like he does in the Foo Fighters. If you listen really closely, it's all the same tune…"

Drew Hester was next in line to be made fun of. Drew was on percussion and vibes. Dave pointed out that playing the triangle was cool; if you were in 3rd grade, not when you're a grown man. Dave said he put ads in newspapers all across America to find an adult male to play triangle in his band. Finally Dave found Drew. Then some dude from the audience yelled out to Dave and said that he played the triangle until he was in 5th grade! Dave chirped back, "Yea and I bet you took the short bus to school too!"

We all knew Dave, so he pretty much skipped his intro and went right to drummer Taylor Hawkins, and yea, he too had a solo—drum solo to be exact—and a bare foot drum solo to be super exact.

After the intros, the group finished the song they were playing when they started the intros.

Between songs, Dave chit chatted with the audience again, which was pretty cool. Dave said that about 12 years ago, the Foos wrote a song and for the music video to that song, they figured that it would be really cool to do a parody of Mentos candy commercials. In retrospect, Dave said it was a very bad idea because fans started to bring Mentos to shows and threw the candy at them whenever they played *Big Me*. So, for the longest time, they shelved the song and refused to play it. Dave said that he hated being hit with Mentos because they were a hard, rock like candy that left him with bruises after shows. He added that they tasted like shit. Dave continued on and said that about two years ago in Canada, they decided to play *Big Me* because it had been years since they played it. So during the song, some dude threw a package of Mentos up on stage, so Dave stopped playing. He said he wanted to go all Hendrix style on the Mentos and light them on fire on stage. Dave searched for his lighter, but he didn't have one, so he asked if anyone in the audience had a lighter. Dave said he was then hit with 1000 cigarette lighters. The next song the Foos played was obviously *Big Me*. Dave had some help on vocals from the violinist Petra.

The rest of the Foos' set consisted of *My Hero, Skin And Bones, Another Round, Over and Out,* and *Cold Day In The Sun*. For *Cold Day In The Sun,* drummer Taylor sang lead vocals.

Afterwards all of the band players left the stage except for Dave. Dave was alone, all by himself on the stage with his black guitar, which Shannon said was a Martin guitar. The stage was entirely black except for the spot light on Dave. "I got another confession to make…I'm your fool…" A solo Dave was singing *Best Of You*.

After *Best Of You,* Dave broke into the first couple notes to their closer *Everlong*. The first part of *Everlong* was played solo by Dave, but during the song the rest of the band took the stage to aid in the finishing of the song.

Once *Everlong* ended, Dave quickly said his thank yous, everyone got up, bowed, exited the stage and the house lights were turned on.

"Huh?! Are you kidding me?! No encore?" I exclaimed! Yes, it was sad but true, there was no encore. The Foos played for about an hour.

Between sets, Shannon and I decided to wander around the place. We ended up finding a concert merchandise booth. $35 for a T-Shirt, no thank you. $20 for a 16x20 poster of Bob Dylan, no thank you…a whole bunch of overpriced shit.

We were going to get a beer, but $10.50 for a 24oz bottle of beer, that was a stab in the balls: I mean that someone took the 24 oz. bottle, smashed it and then stabbed you in the balls with the broken glass…yea.

Eventually Bob Dylan took the stage…horrible, absolutely horrible. My parents raised me with the oldies, so I was exposed to Dylan. I did not mind Dylan's radio played tunes, but he did not play any of his old stuff, just a bunch of new crap that sounded like country. Plus Dylan was not playing guitar, but the key board. It looked like his key board was keeping him upright. And all his new crap sounded exactly the same. I knew Bob had a raspy voice to begin with, but he was just awful…in other words, he should have hung it up years ago. Our ears begin to bleed and I think it was a mix of hearing Bob's emphysema and hacking up a hair ball or him vomiting into the mic. Shannon and I forced ourselves to listen to 30-ish minutes of pain because we were waiting for some good stuff such as *Like A Rolling Stone, All Along The Watch Tower, Knockin' On Heaven's Door* or *Lay, Lady, Lay*. We didn't hear anything we recognized so we booked it. I think Shannon and I were the only ones who were extremely let down by Bob. A dude in the aisle next to us was obviously digging Dylan because he was bobbing his head with his eyes closed.

We left Scotiabank Place at 10pm and it was going to be about 6 hours back to Buffalo…*yuck*.

The ride back to Buffalo sucked as much as Dylan did, maybe even more because at least we were able to run away from Bob.

We made it to the US/Canadian Border in about an hour and a half. It was like Deja vu going over the border…"Adam, where is your birth certificate?" requested the customs officer. "It's at home…in some drawer."

Cornell

Saturday, March 17, 2007, 9:30 A.M...St. Patrick's Day. I was at Cameo's Restaurant doing my usual Saturday morning job there, cleaning up the joint from the drunks the night before...but that day was different. Beside it being St. Patrick's Day, it was also the same day that Chris Cornell tickets went on sale for the Kool Haus in Toronto! I've always wanted to see Soundgarden, but like all of my other favorite bands from the 90's, they were either dead, indisposed, or broken up. On top of that, when my favorite bands were playing back in their hay day, I was like 10 years old. So, I figured that this was my shot to finally see one of my favorite artists.

Saturdays were normally the day that tickets went on sale for music shows; Ticketmaster was no exception. So, there I was, at Cameos, waiting for 10 o'clock to hit and when it finally did, I whipped out my trusty cell phone. I would have used a computer to buy the tickets, but I did not have access to one. I made the call to Ticketmaster and I got through, kind of...I got put on hold, which sucked because my phone started chirping at me because the battery was about to die...and then it did. "Shit!" I said to myself, "Oh well, no big deal, I'll just order them when I get out."

I finally got out of Cameos at 10:30 A.M. After work, I had to go to my girlfriend Shannon's house in Rochester because her family and I we going out to SUNY Potsdam to see Shannon's brother Kyle perform in an opera. I told myself, "Ok, no biggie, I'll just order the tickets for Shannon and me when I get out to her place..."

I made it to Shannon's house before noon and I was on Ticketmaster's web site in no time. I found my artist and venue...I clicked for two tickets, and...SOLD OUT! Mother fucker! Just my luck! I will have you know that I was pretty much pissed and grumpy at myself for the rest of the day. I missed my chance to see Chris Fucking Cornell! There was no way in hell that he would ever come back to the Western New York or Southern Ontario area again...Son of a bitch!

The following week, I was listening to the Canadian rock radio station, 97.7 Hits FM, and the radio DJ was talking about how the Cornell show in Toronto was just awesome. Chris Cornell played stuff from Soundgarden to Audioslave and even played some goodies from Temple of a Dog. That's all I needed to hear, how I missed a great and wonderful, once in a lifetime show. Lord knows none of those three bands will ever reunite, let alone go on a reunion tour…ever!

That summer was shaping up to be extremely boring for concerts. Darien Lake and HSBC Arena were dead, Warped Tour had nobody cool, and the Thursday in the Square in downtown Buffalo had a bunch of no names. That summer was going to suck, until the one day that I opened my email.

My older sister Sarah had sent me a link from one of the Syracuse radio stations. K Rock was sponsoring K Rockathon again that summer. The show included Social Distortion, Evans Blue, Sick Puppies, Drowning Pool, and Deftones with Chris Cornell as the headliner! Fuck Yea! I'm there! So I wasted no time hopping back on shitty Ticketmaster to buy those babies, one for me and of course one for Shannon.

It felt like a decade for Saturday July 21, 2007 to arrive! Shannon and I started our road trip from Rochester to Syracuse at 10:00 in the morning. We hit the road early because gates for the show opened at 11am.

After the hour drive to Syracuse, we met up with Sarah at her house. Like usual, Sarah wasn't at home. She was shopping with the kids, but Guitar Dude (Sarah's husband Eric) was home. So Shannon and I hung out with Guitar Dude for a bit.

I call Eric "Guitar Dude" because he played guitar in the Syracuse based hardcore band Earth Crisis.

It was around noon and Guitar Dude was hungry and Sarah still was not back yet. Guitar Dude asked us if we were hungry, which we were, so we decided to go out for lunch. Sarah and Guitar Dude were vegans, so that meant we couldn't go somewhere normal to eat.

Guitar Dude took us to this place called Alto Cinco. I had no clue where it was because I was not familiar with Syracuse. All I knew was that the food was mad expensive and that I would have killed for some Mighty Taco. Sarah and the kids ended up meeting Guitar Dude, Shannon and me at the restaurant. On Sarah's way over, she stopped at one of the credit unions out there in Syracuse and signed up for a new account. In doing so, she received a pair of tickets to that day's Chris Cornell show.

After we got done eating, I thought that Sarah and Guitar Dude were going to dump the kids off at Guitar Dude's parent's house and then the four of us would go to the show. Apparently I was wrong. We all ended up sitting on the curb outside Alto Cinco, wondering what we were going to do next.

I thought, "I dunno, how about go to the show?!" Sarah was hemming and hawing on whether she wanted to go and Guitar Dude wanted to go to the Syracuse Nationals Car Show that was in Syracuse that weekend. All I knew was that I wanted to see Chris Fucking Cornell!

So about an hour later, we had the troops rallied, and we were on our way to Guitar Dude's parent's house to dump off their rug rats. Guitar Dude's mom was a nurse. She was going to watch the rug rats, Hannah and Jonah, until 11pm because that's when she had to leave for her shift.

Everything was finally going smoothly. Sarah and Guitar Dude were in their Saturn and I was in my trusty '94 Saturn SC2 (the one Sarah gave me the year before) with 170K on the odometer.

The venue for K Rockathon was at the Weedsport Speedway, which I had no clue where it was, or how to get there. Thankfully Sarah and Guitar Dude knew the way, so Shannon and I followed them…from Route 11 to I-81 South to the 90 westbound until we saw out exit for Weedsport.

As we were on the 90, I thought that we were getting pretty close to the show because there was some hippy or homeless looking dude who looked lost; he was wandering in the median of the interstate. Moments later we approached our exit.

The speedway was maybe a mile and a half from the 90.

Parking was scarce; it was pretty much where ever you could find a spot on the back country roads. We ended up parking next to some corn fields. As we downed our 6 cans of Sparks, I told Shannon that we could do it in the corn fields after the show!

We finally made our way up to Sarah and Guitar Dude, who parked behind a 1980s black Buick hearse! I was mortified by dead stuff, but the hearse was pretty cool. If you were wondering, there was no coffin in back.

During our walk to the speedway, we were able to hear Drowning Pool play their last song *Bodies*. I liked *Bodies* because it was a good pump you up song.

As we walked up to security, I told Guitar Dude, "Make sure to turn to the left and cough when they feel you up!"

Soon it was my turn to get felt up by some Buddha butterball rent-a-cop security guard, donned with the cop mustache and no side burns look. Buddha made sure to grab my junk to make sure I was not smuggling anything into the show. I responded to him fondling my unit with a little "Woo-Who!" Buddha did not laugh, but many others did.

After we made it through the gates, I looked around and said, "Holy shit! It's like a huge white trash fest here!" I didn't know what it was…it could have been something in the water, but there were bunches of freaks everywhere…now that I think about it, I'm pretty confident that it wasn't the water they were drinking, judging by the lack of fluoride consumption, everyone there had Summer Teeth, some are here, and some are there.

The four of us walked around for a bit until we eventually sat down on the wooden grandstand bleachers. By that time, it was about 1 or 2, maybe even 3 in the afternoon, and the sun was just beating down hot on everyone. Tell you what, just sitting there and people watching was good! Shannon said it was the best people watching she's ever seen…ever!

There were people totally decked out in Goth…ugly pasty white girls wearing black platform fuck me boots with fish nets and the tiny mini skirt and black top with black and pink hair, with all their white face paint, and mascara running everywhere.

Hillbillies, hicks, white trash, they were a dime a dozen; just everywhere.

There were also some older looking people, like our parents age.

The venue was the Weedsport Speedway, where they had dirt Roundy-round races. There was only one set of long bleachers. The bleacher ran the entire length of one of the straight a ways. If you were sitting on the bleachers, you would be looking at the dirt track. The stage was set up in the inside of the track. If you weren't sitting, then you were standing on the wood chip covered dirt tack. I wasn't sure why the track was covered in wood chips, but maybe it's easier to clean up the puke that way. On the outer perimeter of the track was where all the vendors had set up shop. One of the shops had a huge inflatable creation to attract people to its tent. Shannon said,

"Hey, that's cool, they're giving out ice cream over there!" So Sarah, Guitar Dude, and I looked over to see. We all started to giggle and Shannon asked why we were giggling. I said, "Well, that's not ice cream they are giving away." Shannon looked puzzled and then it clicked that it wasn't a huge inflatable ice cream cone, but a huge Twisted Pleasure Condom…they were giving out free samples!

There were a bunch of shitty bands playing so Sarah and Shannon went to go wander for a bit. Guitar Dude and I hung out, talked, and people watched. Sarah and Shannon came back about 20 minutes later and said that some dude tried selling them a crack pipe. They also said that there was the Hepatitis C tent. Guitar Dude and I looked puzzled, so the ladies took us down to show us. Low and behold, there was a tent where you could pay $10 or $15 to get any body piercing! It definitely did not look healthy or sterile, not to mention that all the piercings took place behind a tarp. No health code certifications were present either.

We wandered around some more on the track and saw some girl that was passed out; face down on the wood chips. It was pretty weird, but the even creepier thing was the increasing number "date rape" guys that began to swarm around her like vultures. Eventually the girl came to and wandered off in a daze.

By that time, Social Distortion was playing. I was not a huge fan of them. The only reason why I knew who they were was because my buddy Jason liked them. As they were playing their set, I recognized one of their songs from the radio, *Ball And Chain*. They also played a cover of the Rolling Stones *Under My Thumb* which was pretty cool. They ended their set with a Johnny Cash cover, *Burning Ring of Fire,* which I liked even better than their Stones cover. After Social D's set was over and the roadies came up on stage, the original Johnny Cash version was played over the PA.

Some more shitty bands played after Social D, and yes, the Deftones were one of those shitty bands. I have been to shows where the Deftones were the opener and I missed them on purpose because they sucked. They should be called the Sucktones or something like that. The first time I saw the Sucktones, they opened for Metallica at the SkyDome in Toronto…and they sucked back then. The second time I saw them, they were an opener at a Family Values tour, but they suck so much that my buddies and I hung out in the parking lot and played beer pong!

So back to today, like usual and not missing a beat, the Sucktones still sucked. The only mildly entertaining part of their set was they broke out in a couple verses of Kelly Clarkson's *Since You've Been Gone* which was actually entertaining. Deftones also played *Change*, but that wasn't their closer. I think their closer was *666* or something stupid like that. The best part of the Sucktones' set was when they finally left the stage!

Ok, I'm going to fast forward a bit and just jump into when Chris Cornell was about to take stage, because that is pretty much the basis of this entire story.

Sarah, Guitar Dude, Shannon, and I made our way down to the track during the last set change. Sarah and Guitar Dude were only going to stay for the first half of the Cornell's set because it was already 9:15-ish and they needed to be back to pick up their kids.

Lights out…Screams…Guitar riffs…Drums pounded on…Lights turned on! The guitar riffs and drums were meshed into harmony to start off *Let Me Drown*. The backup band was on stage except for Chris Cornell.

Soon Cornell rushed out onto the stage as he screamed the intro vocals to *Let Me Drown*. Cornell strolled around the stage in jeans, white shirt, and a black leather coat. Everyone yelled and screamed; the fans on the dirt track were going nuts, everyone was pushing and shoving and jumping and moshing! Empty and filled water bottles could be seen flying towards the stage. One nailed Cornell right in the grill. Crowd surfers began surfing everywhere…it was a fucking mad house!

After *Let Me Drown*, Chris walked across the stage and said, "Wow, there's a lot a crazy mother fuckers out there!" which encouraged the huge mob scene to yell. Chris then told us that another crazy mother fucker was the drummer in his band, and that the drummer grew up not far from where we were; which also got a lot of screams.

I don't really remember what was played next. I want to say that it was *My Wave,* but I may be wrong. After that song, Chris said that he was going to play something from his latest solo record. I thought to myself, I hope this show is not entirely new shit off the new solo record because it wasn't all that great; though there were a couple diamonds in the rough. I was a huge Soundgarden and Audioslave fan, but Cornell's latest solo record *Carry On* was not my favorite. *Carry On* was more of a mellow sounding record. So Chris played some song off that record, I think it might have been *No Such Thing*.

After the solo song and even more crowd surfers, Cornell played a Temple of the Dog tune, *Hunger Strike*. It was so sweet, hearing *Hunger Strike* and seeing the crowd go nuts as more crowd surfers passed by. It was safe to say that almost every surfer that came my way, I was there helping that dude to stay afloat. There were a crap ton of surfers that were dropping like flies.

As Chris performed, he decided to tune it down a bit to mellow the mood with his black acoustic guitar. I would tell you what kind of guitar it was, but when it came to guitar identification, I was like a chick talking about cars…hence it was black and shiny. During the acoustic set, it was only Chris on stage. He began to strum out the first couple chords to *Fell on Black Days. Black Days* was followed up by Audioslave songs *Like a Stone* and *Doesn't Remind Me*. While the acoustic set was short, it was well received.

Moments later, the rest of the backup band was out on stage and they were ripping out the first few notes to *SpoonMan*, one of my favorite Soundgarden songs. Unfortunately they did not do the "spoon clanking solo" during the middle of the song.

As I said before, Shannon is vertically challenged (nothing against her) so I ended up picking her up a couple times during the show so she could see. She was able to get a clear view through some tall people's heads but that was few and far between. A few times I put her on my shoulders so she could see. I knew I wouldn't get yelled at at this concert for doing that because there was no way any security guard could get to us. I wasn't the only dude there whose girl was short. For example, the dude next to us was there with his girl. The girl was probably about 16 or 17-ish. So she went up on her man's shoulders and naturally all the drunk and stoned horny dudes yelled, "Show us your tits" and so she complied…many times. It was especially weird and awkward when some dude my father's age started pushing people out of the way to stare at the broad's boobs.

The rest of the set continued on with a shit ton of moshers and crowd surfers. I have to say that that has been the wildest and craziest concert I've ever been to, and little did I know that there were more antics to come. A couple of the other songs that Cornell and Co. cranked out were *Rusty Cage, Cochise, Outshine, Show Me How to Live,* and *What You Are.*

And then the lights went out and Chris walked off the stage with his band mates. Man, was I pissed! Shannon and I had made our way all the way to the front of the stage for a hand full of songs and then the show was over like that!? And on top of that, they didn't play *Black Hole Sun*! The entire crowd was chanting "Black Hole Sun" for what seemed like five minutes.

Finally Cornell came back out onto the stage and the lights kicked back on. Everyone cheered. Cornell asked if we would like "another one" and the place went crazy. Guitar riffs flared out, it was the beginning heavy, high pitched notes to *Jesus Christ Pose*. A huge mosh pit formed right behind Shannon and me. The place went ape shit! After the song ended and the band left the stage as if they were late for something. The lights to the entire speedway were turned on signifying that the show was over. Man, I thought I was upset before, but no, I was upset more than ever now. The roadies were tossing drum sticks into the crowd along with guitar picks and I was just standing there thinking that I got robbed...they didn't play *Black Hole Sun*! That's like sneezing in front of the Pope and he doesn't say "God bless you". And to top it off, it was only like 10:30pm!!

After everyone cleared the track, Shannon and I found some dude's wallet, so we gave it to security.

When we finally made it out to the parking lot, some dude was chasing after his girlfriend and threatening to beat her, so we tracked down security, again.

We made it to the county road where we parked. Some dudes were lighting off fire crackers in the middle of the road. Another group of kids played their own live concert on their front lawn.

We finally made it to the Saturn. After I turned it over, I realized that I was extremely low on gas, so we stopped at the fueling station that was just down the road. At the fueling station, there were two kinds of people there...if you weren't high or drunk, then you were the pow-pow; the fuzz; the 5.0; the cops. I quickly filled up the tank, trying to not call attention to myself. I gassed up with no problem and we were on our way in no time.

We drove through the tolls to get back on the 90. As we drove around the bend to merge onto the highway, we got stuck behind some car that was doing 15 mph. I looked at Shannon and said, "This ain't good, these dudes are definitely fucked up!" All of a sudden, I saw Crown Vic head lights in my rearview. I said to myself, "I hope that cop doesn't pull me over." It came time to merge onto the highway and the three of us were still doing 15 mph, not 65. So I sling shot past the car, while making sure not to draw attention towards myself and passed the car. After I pulled ahead of the car, I checked my rear view mirror. I could still see the Crown Vic, sitting behind the car I had passed. The two of them were doing about 45 before the cop finally threw the gumballs on.

Shannon and I made it safely back to her parents' house in Rochester.

Foos@ROC

It was Monday July 28, 2008. It was 8am and I had just gotten to work and already the day was dragging!

At the time, I was working maintenance for a group home. All of us maintenance employees were hanging out by our work vans in the parking lot at headquarters, or the "corral" as we commonly referred it. I asked all my coworkers if they were going to see the last greatest rock band, the Foo Fighters, that night at the Blue Cross Arena. They all said, "No", and it was their loss.

Time stood still that entire day because I was so anxious about the Foo Fighters show that night! For once, I did not have to travel all over Hell's Half Acre to see my favorite band. It was nice that they came to me for once!

It seemed like a lifetime before punch out time came at 4:30pm.

I was home by 5pm. I cracked open a beer to commence the pregaming festivities. Shannon and I got ready for the show.

Shannon's parents and grandma, Nana, came and picked us up a little after 6pm. Yes, you heard me correctly; Nana was coming to the Foo Fighters to party with us.

Just a short while later we arrived at the Blue Cross Arena, home of the six time Calder Cup Champions Rochester Americans hockey club.

Before we could get our tickets scanned for the show, we needed to be felt up by security. Shannon got felt up first, then me, and finally my in-laws. When it was Nana's turn, the security guard looked at Nana and said, "Well I guess the Foo Fighters appeals to all generations. Just go on through…"

I looked at my father in law, Jimbo, and said, "What the hell?! How's that work out that Nana doesn't need to be patted down? I'm going to start bringing her to all my concerts. She can sneak in my booze!"

We quickly got situated in our seats in Section 215.

A few minutes later Supergrass took the stage. Up until that night, I had never heard of Supergrass. After hearing them, I couldn't wait until they left the stage because they were taking precious time away from the Foo Fighters.

It felt like an eternity for Supergrass to finish up with their set list.

While the roadies did their thing switching sets, Shannon and I got up to get another round of beer, Molson Canadian to be specific.

As we were getting our beers, we could hear the sound of the bass drum being hammered on, and it wasn't the roadies doing a sound check, but rather Foo Fighters drummer Taylor Hawkins. The fans began to cheer and the opening guitar notes to their new song *Let It Die* rang through the Blue Cross Arena.

The Foo Fighters were touring in support of their latest and sixth studio album, *Echoes, Silence, Patience & Grace*, so it was no surprise that the Foos would be performing a few songs of the new record.

Naturally, the second song the Foo Fighters played was another new song, *The Pretender* which was followed by *Times Like These, No Way Back, Learn to Fly,* and *Cheer Up, Boys (Your Make Up is Running)*.

During the Foos' set, front man Dave Grohl talked to us. He went on a rambling rant and told us that tomorrow when we were at lunch munching down on our cheeseburgers, we would reflect back on this concert and remember how kickass it was and how we needed to tell our friends or coworkers that they missed out on such an awesome kickass show!

The Foo Fighters spiced things up with a cover of Mose Allison's *Young Man Blues*. It was the first time I had ever heard that song; it was different.

Next, the Foos played Shannon's favorite song of the new album, *Long Road to Ruin*.

While the Foo Fighters were playing *Breakout* I looked over to see if Nana was enjoying herself. Sure enough, Nana was sound asleep! I elbowed Shannon to show her that Nana could sleep through anything! I tapped Nana on the shoulder and woke her up. I asked her, "It's not too loud for you, is it?"

Nana said, "No, it's fine."

During the concert, the Foos rocked out and played their extended version of *Stacked Actors*; where during the song, guitarists Dave Grohl and Chris Shiflett had a jam and shredding session, which was followed up with a drum solo by Taylor Hawkins, and then the band jumped back into finishing *Stacked Actors.*

The Foos slowed things down a bit and went acoustic for a few songs: *Skin and Bones, Marigold,* and *My Hero.* In between songs, Dave talked to us and told us that the Foo Fighters were going to be on a Top Chef's Thanksgiving special. They just recorded it that day in Rochester and it will air on Bravo during Thanksgiving! Then Dave gave out introductions of each of the band members. The Foos ended their acoustic set with *Cold Day in the Sun* with drummer Taylor Hawkins on lead vocals.

After the acoustic set, the Foo Fighters jumped back into the noise and head banging with *Everlong.* I was a little nervous that *Everlong* may have been the last song of the night because *Everlong* has been known to be the band's closing song, but thankfully it was not the case that night in Rochester!

The Foos played my favorite, *Monkey Wrench.*

In between songs, some dude in the crowd at the front of the stage kept yelling at Dave to play Elton John's *Tiny Dancer* (Years ago, Dave was on Craig Kilborn's late night show, and performed a rendition of *Tiny Dancer.* It was comical—but good). From the stage Dave looked at the fan and asked if the guy really wanted to hear *Tiny Dancer.* Everyone in the Blue Cross Arena cheered because they wanted to hear it. Dave told us that he was going to play *Tiny Dancer* and the fans cheered louder. It turned out that Dave lied to us and played *All My Life* instead. I don't think the fans minded too much because *All My Life* is a huge fan favorite.

And with that, the Foos ended their set, and left the stage…or so we thought.

But thankfully they came back for the ritual encore.

They kicked things off old school with *Big Me.* As soon as I heard the opening melody to *Big Me*, I turned to Shannon and told her, "Damnit! I forgot to bring Mentos to throw at the guys on stage!"

Shannon said, "It's ok, maybe next time. Plus we are too far away to throw Mentos."

The Foo Fighters had another surprise for us. They brought out Supergrass' lead singer Gaz Coombes to sing vocals on their cover of the Who's *Bargain.*

The Foos officially ended their encore and evening with *Best of You.*

Shannon and I both agreed that we just witnessed a great Foo Fighters show—not only did they spice things up with a couple covers, but they played at least one song from all six of their albums!

As the family exited Blue Cross Arena, Shannon and I wanted to check out the merchandise table. Shannon and I both honed in on a t-shirt for Nana! For sale was the pink colored "I heart Dave Grohl" t-shirt that was featured in the Foo's music video for *Long Road to Ruin* (if you don't know what I'm referring to, just look up the music video online, it's funny and well worth your time).

Nana thanked Shannon and me for buying her a concert shirt.

The following day when I was at lunch, I reflecting back on last night's concert and Dave's words. Though I was not eating a cheeseburger, he was correct on how awesome that show was. Unfortunately my coworkers didn't care about the Foo Fighters, but that didn't stop me from bragging about the kickass show.

A few days later, Nana found a pair of pink pants that matched her "I heart Dave Grohl" t-shirt! Nana rocked that outfit about once a week all summer long! It was quite the conversation starter at the family reunion! The family was pleasantly shocked to find out that we took Nana to a Foo Fighters concert and that she enjoyed it.

Months later it was Thanksgiving and time for Top Chef's Thanksgiving special featuring the Foo Fighters. Now I'm not sure of all the legalities and copywrites, so I'm not sure if I'm at liberty to give accounts or descriptions of the episode…but what the hell, I'll give Bravo and Top Chef some free advertisement!

Top Chef was your typical cooking show where contestant chefs battle each other in a game show. Season 5, Episode 3 took place in Rochester, NY. A whole bunch of contestants had to cook a Thanksgiving style meal for the Foo Fighters, who were special guest judges.

Each contestant got to run through a local grocery store and pick out food items…Sorry Danny Wegman, but the show's producer chose the other locally owned grocer, Hegedorns in Webster, NY. It was pretty cool of Bravo to advertise a mom-n-pops store on TV.

Next, the chefs were brought downtown to the Blue Cross Arena. With the beautiful city skyline and Genesee River in the back ground, the chefs were battling the clock to finish their Thanksgiving dinners for the Foos. The Fighters of Foo enjoyed their Thanksgiving dinner before their Rochester concert. They discussed what dishes they liked, disliked, and what could be better.

I won't give any secrets away on how each chef did, though at the end of the episode, they did feature a few snippets of the concert.

Shannon and I thought everything was awesome! First the Foo Fighters concert was kick ass. Second it was cool that Top Chef featured Rochester and the Foo Fighters on national TV. Third we didn't have to take a long road trip to see the Foos.

Collective Soul

To celebrate our one year wedding anniversary, Shannon and I flew out to Las Vegas to renew our wedding vows with Elvis. Shannon's parents and Nana flew out along with my mom to take part in the ceremony.

The Elvis wedding was awesome and the Vegas vacation was a blast.

On the last night of our trip, Shannon and I had tickets to see Collective Soul at pool side at the Hard Rock Café Casino.

I wasn't too sure of the attire that we were allowed to wear. I know the show was advertised at "pool side" so I wasn't sure if we could wear swim suits or what. When we first entered the Hard Rock Casino, there was a sign that read, "dress code strictly enforced" so I wasn't sure if we needed to be dressed half way decently or what. But regardless, Shannon and I played it safe and went a little dressy.

Once we arrived at the Hard Rock, the place was a mob scene. There was a huge line of cars that spilled out onto the road, and were blocking traffic. Inside the casino was a zoo. Shannon and I finally found the line for the show, and the line wrapped half way around the casino floor.

After waiting a while, we finally made it through security, and then outside to the pool. Everyone there was wearing swim suits and partying it up in the water. Oh well, I guess we'll know for next time that we can wear swim suits for a pool side concert.

Because Shannon and I were parched, we soon found ourselves in the beer line (I think a mild form of Purgatory is waiting in a beer line at a rock concert or sporting event because it takes so damn long to get your beers).

Finally it was our turn in line. Shannon and I both ordered two Coronas. The bartender came back with 4 luke warm canned beers with a price tag of $28! Holy shit! $28 for four beers?! You gotta be shitting me! For $28 I could walk across the street to CVS and buy two 30 packs worth of beer, but Shannon and I were land locked. Desperate times called for desperate measures, so I coughed up the $28. It would take a 2nd mortgage to get drunk at a rock concert there

After we got our beers, Shannon and I walked around the pool and through the maze of people. We found some tiki hut that had a flight of stairs behind it. The stairs went up and behind the main stage. Shannon and I attempted to go up the stairs, but we were soon met by a bouncer. The bouncer asked if we had tickets and I told him that we did. He asked to see them, so I showed him. The bouncer looked at them and said that they were just the general admission tickets, not the VIP tickets. I pulled a green back from my pocket and said, "George Washington says I have VIP tickets." The bouncer laughed and told me to keep it moving.

Shannon and I soon found a nice place to stand…right in a garden that was pool side. Shannon loved seeing concerts, but she unfortunately suffered from Short Person Syndrome, and without fail, the tallest person **ALWAYS** stood in front of her. However, in the garden was a pretty big rock. Standing on the rock helped to relieve Shannon of her Short Person Syndrome.

There was an opener, and like most openers, I don't remember their name because they sucked. As we suffered through the opener, Shannon and I noticed that not only were we the youngest people there, but we were the most overdressed and most sober too.

A couple ended up standing in front of Shannon, but thanks to her rock, she could still see. However, the broad in front of us could barely stand up due to major alcohol consumption. Hey, I'm not gonna lie, we've all been there before, so I wasn't going to hold that over the broad's head. However, as the show progressed, the chick got worse and kept falling into Shannon.

Shannon asked me, "Can I just punch her? I'll knock her out in one punch. She's belligerent and drunk! She's only fallen into me 5 times! Just let me punch her!"

I told Shannon, "You can't punch her."

Shannon asked, "Why not? You don't think I can take her?"

I replied, "No, I think you can take her, but Collective Soul hasn't even taken the stage yet. Tell you what; you can knock her out once Collective Soul takes the stage."

It was well after 10pm, almost 10:30 by the time Collective Soul took the stage and every one cheered. The stage was nice and simple, nothing flashy. There were multi colored lights up on stage, but that was it; no frills.

Collective Soul put on a great show and they sounded great live. They played all their old classics such as *Heavy, She Said, Precious Declaration,* and *Energy.*

The show was pretty much a "greatest hits" show, but they were also plugging their latest album *Collective Soul (Rabbit)*, which was released the month before. Off the new album, they played *Staring Down.*

As the first few guitar riffs of *Shine* were strummed out, the whole place went crazy. The swimmers in the pool jumped up and down, the people pool side went wild, the people on the upper deck cheered, while the people whose hotel rooms over looked the pool got a free show. And they probably had unlimited beer from their beer runs to CVS.

During Collective Soul's set, the drunk broad in front of us was being fed more cocktails and swaying even more. She had fallen into Shannon a few more times, and Shannon leaned back to me and said, "Ok, I'm liking the show and music and my spot on the rock. Maybe I won't punch her. I think I'll just push her…you know, help her along, to the floor, and then I can see better!"

A few seconds later, the broad fell back into Shannon and Shannon shoved the broad back where she came from. The broad's boyfriend caught her before she face planted. The broad turned around and didn't know who to yell at or punch. The boyfriend calmed down the broad and told Shannon and me that the broad was one tough girl and that she had been to Woodstock '99, so she could hold her own. As Shannon's fist clenched, she snapped back and barked, "She can't hold her own, and she can barely stand up!"

I told Shannon, "Well, if she falls into you again, you can punch her."

Shannon replied, "No, I'm enjoying the show too much to let this dumb fuck ruin it for me."

Moments later, the drunk broad stumbled backwards, yet again. As the broad fell back, she attempted to grab a hold of Shannon to break her fall, but Shannon simply stepped to the side. The drunk broad's boyfriend quickly picked her up and helped her back onto her feet while Shannon grinned and giggled at me.

Collective Soul also played *Why Pt.2, Listen, December,* and a couple other songs I can't remember. I think they also might have played *Where the River Flows.*

In between songs, lead man Ed Roland talked to the crowd and told us how he and his brother/band mate Dean Roland grew up outside Atlanta, GA. They were sons of a minister and touched on life growing up with him. *Gel* was influenced by their dad and dedicated the song to him; they played *Gel* next.

Collective Soul came back out for an encore which started with the stage lights all out. All that could be heard was a few chords from an acoustic guitar, and then a silhouette of a man walking up onto the stage. The man with the guitar was lead man Ed Roland and he began to play the first few notes of *The World I Know* and everyone cheered and whipped out their lighters and cell phones. Ed didn't jam right into the song though. He played the opening notes until the rest of the band walked back on stage. Once they got into their places and picked up their instruments, Ed started singing *"Has our conscience shown? Has the sweet breeze blown? Has all the kindness gone?"* And with everyone with beer, light or cell phone in hand sang back, *"Hope still lingers on. I drink myself of newfound pit Sitting alone in New York City And I don't know why..."* Ed played and sang the rest of the song, while having 2000+ back up singers with him. As the song ended, the band left the stage, but Ed was still up there playing the last few notes on repeat. Ed waited for the band to fully exit, and the stage lights went out. Ed exited the stage, with the last few notes fading into the background.

After the show let out, Shannon and I were forced to walk back into the casino gaming floor and I think there were more people in there than before the concert. It turned out that Hard Rock had another show going on as well. Santana was the other act, but I was not a Santana fan, so I didn't miss out.

By then, Shannon and I had the midnight munchies, so we walked around for a bit, but ended up opting on one of the restaurants in the casino, Mr. Lucky's 24-7.

After food, Shannon and I decided to call it a night because our flight back home was the next morning.

Alice in Toronto-land

Let me take you back in time to where Guidos were sportin' new Camaro IROCs right off the assembly line, the Buffalo Bills were in the Super Bowls, and grunge was the music of the day. Yes that's right, I'm talking about the early 1990s, and if you're still wondering what IROC stood for, it's not International Racing of Champions, but rather Italian Retard Out Cruzin' (PS-I'm Italian…I'm allowed).

Last weekend, I took Shannon up to Toronto to see one of my all-time favorites and one of the best grunge bands—Alice in Chains! But before I dive right into last Saturday night, I think I should give you some background story to go along with it.

I was a huge Alice in Chains fan and in high school I played the shit out of all their CDs until they were beyond scratched. I know I'm dating myself, but I remember back in my senior year of high school, lead singer Layne Staley died due to a heroin overdose. I'm sure if you asked Forrest Gump, he would probably say something like, "Layne sang too many songs and just woke up dead one day. He died on a Tuesday, and that's alls I gots to say about that." Any who, it sucked learning that Layne died and knowing that I would never see one of my favorite all time bands.

Well, let's fast forward from 2002 to 2005. The surviving band members got the band back together…they were probably broke or something. And just like in *Blues Brothers 2000*, when Jake Blues was replaced by John Goodman, Layne Staley was replaced by William DuVall.

Shortly after getting the band back together, Alice in Chains went on tour and I finally got to see them. Back in 2007, they opened for Velvet Revolver at Darien Lake. The band teased me, they only played for 45 minutes. Don't get me wrong, it was an awesome set and they sounded great, but I just wanted them to play longer! It was kind of like on New Year's Eve when you weren't legal and you have some champagne and start rocking a nice buzz and then your parents sweep in, cock block you, and take away the booze.

The rest of the concert went well too. I got to see Scott Wieland, the lead singer of Velvet Revolver. Scott was a phenomenal singer and always put on a great stage show

With AIC back together, a new lead singer, and a tour already underway, this only meant one thing. The band had to record some new material! Well, who says hell doesn't freeze over, 'cause in September of 2009, Alice in Chains finally released a new CD…their first studio album in 14 years! I was a little nervous that *Black Gives Way to Blue* was going to suck. However, much to my surprise and enjoyment, the album rocked. It was hard, heavy, dark, angry, and loud.

Anyway, back to the story. So after getting that little concert teaser from Alice in Chains, I knew that I had to go see them again, no matter where they were playing. The next show within driving distance was Saturday September 18, 2010 in downtown Toronto at the Molson Amphitheater: a venue overlooking Lake Ontario.

A few days before the show, I told my coworker Ian that I was going up to Toronto to see Alice in Chains. He corrected me by saying, "No you're not. You're going up to see an Alice in Chains *Cover Band*…Wait, didn't the lead singer die like 10 years ago? What song is this and who am I?...*I'm the man in the box, buried 6 feet under!* Ha!" and Ian went on to make more jokes about the band. I asked Ian if this new revised Alice in Chains was like when David Lee Roth left Van Halen and Sammy Hagar took over the band to make it "Van Hagar." Ian was still adamant that this was only an *Alice in Chains Cover Band.*

Well, any who, Shannon and I left Rochester around 2pm. On a good day, it takes about three hours to get to Toronto and that was if all the moons are aligned, such as no wait at the border and no God awful traffic in downtown Toronto. Well, apparently the moons were aligned because we hit downtown a little after 5pm.

Shannon and I did not want to get too shit faced because we wanted to remember the show, plus we were going to crash at my mom's in Buffalo for the night. So with that being said, we were going to limit our beerverage consumption, and that was why we only brought up four Tilts with us, two tall 24 ounce cans a piece.

Since it was barely 5:30 and we were the only ones in the parking lot for the concert. We didn't want to polish off our four drinks, so we went wandering in downtown, in search of the closest watering hole.

It only took us about 6 blocks, but we soon found Guirei Japanese Restaurant, a Sushi Bar at 600 Queens Quay West.

Shannon was happy and excited because she loves Sushi; but me, not so much. I was more of a pizza and wings kind of guy, but they had beer here at this Sushi Bar. And good beer too! I liked Canadian made beer because it was none of that pussy ass, low alcohol content beer we had back here in the States.

For dinner, I started off with a local Toronto brew, Steam Whistle, before moving on to a Molson. Shannon had a Steam Whistle and then followed it up with a Red Rickards. Shannon ended up ordering some fish sushi roll wrap which tasted like fishy crap. Tell you what, if you put some Franks Red-hot on that shit, it would have been good. Now me, I had the bacon scallops. I'm not going to lie, bacon makes everything taste wonderful. Eventually 7 pm rolled around and we needed to bust a move.

We soon found ourselves back in the parking lot in my '03 Chevy Impala. Shannon and I were tailgating inside the car, pounding down our Tilt. Yes, you heard me correctly; we were tailgating inside the car. Even though Canada is Heaven for making good beer, you were not allowed to tailgate in Toronto!

While we pregamed some more, I hoped AIC would play one of my other favorite songs, *Queen of the Rodeo*, its lyrics still rang through my head...*I drink too much, I smoke too much, I'm a human waste. I buy a lot of cheap alcohol honey, but I really hate the taste!*

As soon as we finished our Tilts, we were on our way for our short walk to the Molson Amphitheater. I knew Black Diamond Skye was the opener, but Shannon and I didn't have any real ambition to see them; hence the drinking in the car.

It took us forever to get into the amphitheater because there were only three gates open and security was taking their sweet ass time groping people down. While waiting in line, Shannon and I learned that the Deftones were the second opener of the night. I was a little pissed off because that meant that the shitty Deftones were taking more stage time away from Alice in Chains. So once Shannon and I were molested by the security guards, we passed through the turn styles. Once inside there was only one thing to do to help ease the pain of being tormented by the Deftones...and that was to get another round of that wonderful Molson Canadian beer. Tell you what, a few rounds of Molson later, the Deftones didn't suck as much, but they were still pretty shitty.

In the meantime, while Shannon and I were killing time during the Deftones set, we wandered over to the merchandise table. I was tempted to get a shirt or something until I saw the prices. The cheapest Alice in Chains T-shirt was $35! Damn! You had to be kidding me, $35! Apparently someone had to pay for Alice's drug addictions and it was every SAP that we saw walking around with a current concert tour shirt!

It started to drizzle a little bit, so Shannon and I decided to wander over to our seats. Our seats were located in the last section underneath the pavilion section, but they were not covered by the canopy. It was ok though, because the rain helped fill up our beer cups to give us the illusion that we were drinking light beer.

Finally the Deftones finished up. That was our cue to pee and buy another round of beer. By the time we got back to our seats, we realized that we were on our 4th or 5th round of beer...maybe? You know that Canadian beer has a higher octane than American beer; it had that extra 1-2 punch. We vaguely remembered that we were going to keep the drinking to a two round limit...maybe we meant that only for the Sushi Bar.

It felt like forever for the stage crew to switch the Deftones crap over to Alice in Chains' gear. During the process, people were yelling and cheering in anticipation for Alice.

All of a sudden the lights went out and screams echoed throughout the amphitheater. Soon there were lights shining from the back of the stage through a huge cloth that draped across the front of the stage; only the silhouette of the drum set could be seen, distortion of a guitar and strained voices were heard. Then the "Fall Out Shelter" logo was displayed upon the draped cloth, with noise growing louder. Eventually a heart (from the cover of Alice's newest album) pumped in beat over the fall out logo. A trippy light show then ensued upon the draped cloth, while being able to see the band take to stage. With much anticipation, the cloth finally dropped when William DuVall dropped out the first "AHH!" to *Them Bones*, and the place went fuckin' crazy! *Them Bones* was followed up by *Dam That River*.

Before the show, I was hoping that Alice in Chains wasn't going to play a "greatest hits" show because they have too many other good songs to play other than their radio hits. At the same time too, I was hoping they were not going to play every song off their new album. Don't get me wrong, the new stuff was great, but like every other established band, everyone wants to hear all of the old shit! And tell you what, Alice in Chains did not disappoint!

Alice in Chains did play some songs off their new album such as *Check My Brain, Last of My Kind, Lesson Learned,* and one of their slow numbers, *Your Decision.*

They spiced it up by playing some rare shit off their debute album Facelift, *It Ain't Like That.*

Alice in Chains pumped out some great classic tunes such as *Again, We Die Young, Rain When I Die,* and *Grind.* Then, they slowed things up for a bit to blast out a soft tune, and one of my absolute favorites, *No Excuses.*

Heaven forbid, what would an Alice in Chains show be without *the* song based on and dedicated to the co-founder and lead guitarist Jerry Cantrell's dad? Yea, that's fricking right, they played *Rooster*! The song that is a tribute to, and about, an American Hero, that was sent off to Vietnam to fight for his country. It is about a man who was sent off from his family to fight in war, a man that watched all his friends die at war, a man that came back from war to an America that shit on him for serving his country. During the whole song, the band played the music video to *Rooster*, which featured the Rooster himself, Mr. Cantrell.

Alice in Chains came back on stage for a much expected encore. Their encore started with William DuVall coming out on stage and telling us that they only had time for a couple more songs and "to take this house strong, man." DuVall could not finish his sentence before the guitarist Jerry Cantrell, bassist Mike Inez, and drummer Sean Kenny broke into one of the band's top and most famous hit, *Man In The Box.* The place went hysterical; people jumping around everywhere; with people yelling and screaming every word to *Man In The Box.* Even down to the emphasis of shouting the word "shit" in "*buried in my SHIT!*"

Man In The Box was followed up by one of my all-time favorite Alice in Chains songs, *Nutshell.* I was so excited and amazed that Alice played *Nutshell.* It was one of those acoustic and quiet songs that I thought I would never hear the band play live. Cantrell, with electric guitar at hand, was facing DuVall with acoustic guitar at hand. They were being illuminated by a spot light on a pitch black stage. Soon, DuVall and Cantrell's voices echoed dark and pained opening notes to the song.

The show ended with one of their other biggest songs, *Would*.

Though they had too many great songs to play in such little time, they chose a solid set list.

And like that, the show was over. And like the first time I saw them, they left me yearning for more. I wanted Alice in Chains to play more. There was so much more to be heard. Without fail, every time I see a great show, somehow the Deftones fudge it up and steal time away from the headliner, like the times when I saw Metallica, Korn, and Chris Cornell.

Once the show ended, we thought that traffic would be heavy, so we just strolled around the amphitheater grounds a bit before we stumbled upon the Voodoo Garden bar. We didn't have anything better to do, so we entered the multi-level rooftop bar where we soon found ourselves nursing some more overpriced concert beer.

By the time we got back to the car, it was midnight and the two of us were very sleepy. We had a long day. I was up at 6am for work, and didn't get out of work until noon. On top of that, I was coming down with a cold.

Shannon and I soon hopped onto the QEW to head back to Buffalo. I think we made it to Mississauga before we pulled off to take a catnap in a motel parking lot. I couldn't really afford a room at the motel considering I was a broke college student.

Well, it was still pitch black at 5am when I awoke from my slumber. Surprisingly enough, the Impala was pretty comfortable for sleeping. But then, Shannon and I had a new mission on our hands. We needed to stop off at Duty Free at the border crossing to restock on rations.

We finally pulled into the Duty Free at the Queenston/Lewiston Bridge at 6am. Now I know that I had been touting how delicious Canadian beer is, but there was one gem that Canada keeps hidden. It was hidden so well that they didn't even sell this beer in the bars up there in the North Country, and you can only obtain this at Duty Free and the Beer Store. And that would be Canada's best tasting beer, Molson Brador. And yes, that malt beverage was quite potent; you have 3 or 4 of these and it slams you on your ass. Shannon picked up some Rickard's Red because that was her favorite Canadian brew.

We finally made it to my mom's by 6:30am, where Shannon and I continued our catnap.

STP, the band not the motor oil company

Not only was Saturday May 7th, 2011 my Nana's 92 birthday (may God rest her soul), but it was also the same day that Stone Temple Pilots were playing in Rochester, NY at the Main Street Armory. And for once, Shannon and I did not have to road trip for another rock concert.

Now I know that if I've said it once, then I've said it a thousand times, but Stone Temple Pilots lead singer Scott Weiland was always in my Death Pool. Scott is one of the last great performers from the 1990s rock scene and has somehow managed to stay alive with all the heroin and other drugs he has done.

I have to say that STP was one of the last great '90s drug bands that has somehow managed to stay alive…and for all you who are rolling their eyes and bitching, *"What about Pearl Jam, Phish, or Dave Mathews Band?"* Well, my only response to that would have to be a quote from Bob Saget's character in the movie *Half Baked*, when Bob blurted out at a rehab meeting, "Weed?! Weed's not a drug. You never see anyone suck dick for weed…" Hence I rest my case.

A few years back, it broke my heart when STP broke up. I was sad and upset that such a great band was no more. On top of that, I never got to see them play.

Eventually Scott Weiland joined the remaining guys from Guns-n-Roses to form Velvet Revolver. The DeLeo brothers went off and did their own side project, but it never took off like Velvet Revolver.

Eventually Velvet Revolver broke up and Scotty boy found himself out of work. Then history seemed to repeat itself in the form of *Blue Brothers*…get the band back together. I highly doubt Stone Temple Pilots were on a mission from God, but rather a mission for money or more heroin. Either way, I was thrilled that STP got back together.

Once STP got back together, they embarked on a summer long tour in 2009. One of those stops on their schedule happened to be at CMAC in Canandaigua, NY; translation, it was only a 45 minute hike for Shannon and me to see them. The STP show at CMAC was awesome, though it was primarily a greatest hits show.

However, after STP finished up their summer tour, they hit up the recording studio. Apparently while on tour, STP started writing new material.

In 2010, STP released their self-titled album, *Stone Temple Pilots*.

Ok, so now we are back up to speed with the days leading up to May 7th, 2011. A couple of Rochester's radio stations were giving away free concert tickets. I however couldn't win a pair.

One of the radio stations that were giving tickets away was the Zone @ 94.1, Rochester's New Rock Station. The Zone bragged how they played "new, fresh, stank free rock first" and the Zone was advertising the STP show on their air waves.

A couple clicks down on the radio dial, 96.5 WCMF, Rochester's Classic Rock Station was also advertising and giving away free tickets to STP.

I'm not going to lie, I felt a little weird and had a little dilemma going on inside my head…**am I old?!** I had to weigh out the differences and evaluate my situation. Yea, the new rock station played STP and was giving away free tickets. On the other hand, the classic rock station was *only* giving away STP tickets, they did not play STP over their airwaves. So, being the sleuth that I was, I figured that I was still "young" because all the 90s bands I grew up listening to were still played on the new rock stations, not the classic rock stations.

A few days before the show, Shannon and I still had to go pick up our tickets. We ended up purchasing our tickets from the Great House of Guitars, commonly known as the HOG.

Whenever Shannon visited the House of Guitars, she became a kid in a candy store and got lost in the HOG's vast selection of guitars. The HOG had it all from autographed electric guitars, to acoustic, to electric acoustic guitars. Not to mention they did have a lengthy selection of acoustic and electric ukuleles. And they also had drum sets and amps and all that other stuff…but that's just on the main floor.

Once you walk through the instrument section, you venture up a set of steps, down the hallways, past the drums and amps—that are stacked from floor to ceiling—then you walk down a flight of stairs, through a heavy metal door, and then you are in the music section of the House o Guitars. According to the HOG, they were the

World's Largest Music Store, and I would have believed it. They have everything from Rap and R&B, to Oldies, to Rock, to Classical, to Show tunes. And all these genres can be found in either 45s, vinyl albums, cassettes, CDs, DVD, and even though I didn't see them, they probably had 8 Tracks. And aside from all the music, which was an organized mess, they also have a huge selection of concert shirts. Even the ceiling was loaded with old concert and album promo posters. The pillars that held up the ceiling had autographed pictures and albums of famed music legends that had visited to the HOG; such as Ozzy Osborne, Paul McCartney, and Sammy Hagar, just to name a few.

In the far, nether region, off to a corner in the HOG was a and Ticket Fly hub, where Shannon and I purchased our tickets…$80 presale for the pair. I thought to myself, "Shit man! 80 bucks!? This better be one kick ass show…"

Ok, so now we are up to speed with Saturday May 7, 2011.

Like many concerts before, Shannon and I decided to pregame a little bit before the show, just so we weren't dropping $50 or $100 bucks on beer at the show.

Since the show was being played in downtown Rochester, I was feeling a little hometown pride, so I kicked off the pregame festivities with a local "River Water" brew; I had a Genesee Beer. Genny, had been brewed in Rochester, NY since 1878.

Once Shannon and I got to the Main Street Armory, we parked on some side street to continue with our pregame. Even though the doors opened at 7pm and it was already 7:30pm, Shannon and I opted on killing a few more beers in the Chevy Impala…and no, it wasn't a cool muscle car Impala, but rather a boring, plain Jane 2004 Impala.

After we killed our beers, it was time to head into the Armory.

On our three block walk to the Armory, I had to break the seal. I somehow inherited my mother's bladder…that meant I had to pee every 30 seconds.

Thankfully there was a Wendy's on the way that we stopped at. It was good for two reasons. First of all, I could pee and second of all, Shannon and I could finally try Wendy's new Naturally Cut Fries, because you know, *according to a national taste test survey,*

*Wendy's Naturally Cut Fries beat out McDonalds' fries…*or at least that's what their commercials said.

Surprisingly there was a line for the men's room and no line for the women's room…so I piddled in the women's room…and yes, I put the toilet seat back down…and yes, I washed my hands for 30 seconds with soap, water, and friction.

Shannon and I agreed that Wendy's new fries were good, but we still preferred McDonalds fries.

Before long, Shannon and I were at the steps to the Main Street Armory and we were getting our hands stamped for beer. Then we walked up the huge concrete steps, and inside the 100+ year old Armory.

The Main Street Armory was built back in 1905 and has seen the service men of World War I and II pass through its doors. Back in the day, the Armory use to be the host of car shows and local Rochester sports (http://rochestermainstreetarmory.com).

I had been to the Armory a couple times before. I took Shannon there for registration when she ran the Rochester Half Marathon. Also my father in law, Jimbo, and I saw amateur boxing there a few years back.

Once Shannon and I were inside the venue, we headed right over to the beer line! Apparently great minds thought alike because almost everyone in the Armory was in the beer line. Shannon and I were amazed at the beer prices, $4 per beer! *Holy crap, for a rock concert, was beer cheap!* We both ordered two rounds of Labatt Blue Light Lime, and even though Labatt is a Canadian beer, the Lime version was brewed down the street at the Genesee Brewery

While we were in line for beer, Shannon and I noticed the stage. The backdrop on the stage was Stone Temple Pilots flower logo. Now Shannon and I did not know if there was an opener. All the ads on the radio did not advertise a special guest or opener, so we were hoping for a three hour long STP set.

As we were in line for beer, the opener came on. I had never heard of the group before, but ladies and gentlemen, let me introduce to you Rose Hill Drive. And to be quite honest with you, they didn't suck, and I was quite amazed that they were half way decent. They looked like they were having fun and enjoying themselves. Shannon bought their CD at the end of the show. All the guys in the band, except one of the guitarists, looked just like Jesus, with the long hair and beards. They should have renamed the band *The Jesus Trio* or *The Holy Trinity* or something like that.

As Rose Hill Drive played, I had to pee again. Now it had been some time since I've been to the Armory that I forgot how cool their bathrooms are. Since the Armory was built back in 1905, there was a lot of thought, craftsmanship, and quality that went into the construction of those old buildings. The floors in the bathroom still had the original tile/mosaic floor and the stalls had beautifully hand crafted hard wood partitions and doors. The doors to the shitters were especially cool because they were like the double swinging doors in the saloons in the Wild West.

During Rose Hill Drive's set, there was some dude behind Shannon and me that was high or tripping on something good. This dude was all into the opener. His arms were flailing in the air as if he was at some traveling salvation gospel revival tour. Needless to say the dude ended up face planting hard onto the solid wood floor. I thought it was pretty funny, so I just laughed.

Shannon noticed that half of the windows in the Armory had been bricked over and the remaining windows were red in color. Shannon leaned towards me and pointed it out and expressed her fear, "I've read a lot of Ann Rice and that Twilight (crap) and think that in like 5 minutes, the band is going to turn into vampires and fly around and the doors are gonna be locked and it's gonna turn into a huge blood bath."

Eventually Rose Hill Drive thanked us and STP right before they played their closing song. That was cue for Shannon and me to head over to the bathrooms before the mad rush.

I still did not understand why it took forever for the roadies to change sets. Why must it take at least 30-60 minutes to swap everything out? It was their job, wouldn't you figure that they would have it down to a science and crank out the set change in like 20 minutes? Anyway, the set change probably took about 30-45 minutes.

The house lights went out and screams and chants of "STP" could be heard.

Enter Stone Temple Pilots!

The DeLeo brothers entered the stage with their guitars and flanked out to opposite ends of the stage. Eric took his spot behind his drums and lead man Scott came out looking like a Reservoir

Dog; white dress shirt and black tie, pants, and jacket. Scott took his place, front and center, standing on a large set of speakers, with megaphone at hand.

The band kicked off their set with *Crackerman* and the Armory went crazy. Even though Shannon and I were on the younger end of the spectrium of fans there to see STP, it did not stop the older folk from crowd surfing, there were a lot of them, and it lasted throughout the whole show!

STP followed up *Crackerman* with *Heaven & Hot Rods*. The whole place was wild and full of energy and everyone singing every line of every song. I'm not gonna lie, the band should have recorded the show for a live album or something, because the band sounded great and the fans were stoked.

Stone Temple Pilots played a couple songs from their latest self-titled release, which I didn't mind because it's a good record; *Between the Lines* and *Hickory Dichotomy* were the tracks.

Shannon noticed some broad in front of us who was wearing sandals. Shannon leaned to me and said, "She's an amateur concert goer, hence the sandals. Did she not notice the other chikas who are wearing the four inch stilettos here? Not a good mix; those stilettos are gonna find those sandals and it's not gonna be pretty…"

STP had a little bass and guitar jam session that lasted about a minute or two, which turned out to be a very long intro to *Vasoline*.

It got extremely hot standing there in the pit, but I could only imagine how hot it got up on stage. Scotty boy eventually took off his coat and half way through the show, he had already sweated through his dress shirt. I was hoping for some classic Scott Weiland, where he's half naked or almost completely naked on stage.

The crowd went crazy for every song STP sang, whether it was *Meat Plow, Wicked Garden, Down, Still Remains,* or *Silvergun Superman.*

In between songs, Scott told the fans, "Here's another song we do that a lot of people think we wrote, but we didn't…we'll still take credit for it any way…" The band then played a cover of Led Zeppelin's *Dancing Days* and the crowd just ate it up while more crowd surfers were tossed up.

Plain and simple, Stone Temple Pilots was putting on a phenomenal show and even played the little instrumental ditty, *Press Play*, before breaking into one of their other songs. In between songs, they also played the first couple notes of *And So I Know* before breaking into a completely different STP tune.

STP even played *Big Empty*, which Shannon absolutely loved! Shannon said, "I have no idea what he's singing about and it all sounds like mumbling gibberish, so I can make up my own lyrics to sing along!"

Scott told the crowd that their next song was written by bass guitarist Robert DeLeo, while Rob was working in a guitar store. The entire Armory went insane went the first few chords of *Plush* were jammed out. I like when groups give a little history lesson to their songs because you never find that in the liner notes to the albums.

STP also played *Lounge Fly, Interstate Love Song,* and *Trippin' On a Hole in a Paper Heart.* Scott's stage performance was great, but he wasn't bouncing around on stage like I had seen in previous shows. Don't get me wrong, he was still good, but he wasn't the drugged out marching band leader/pole dancer that I had become accustomed to seeing.

Stone Temple Pilots came back out for a two song encore, in which they played *Dead and Bloated* and *Sex Type Thing*. The house lights came on and the band took center stage, bowed, and Scott thanked all the fans for their support and thanked their road crew. The band called a few "behind the scenes" members out on stage and thanked them personally.

And with that, the show was over. STP had probably played for an hour and a half, and like any other good show I've seen, I wished that they would have played even longer.

Shannon and I soon found ourselves at the merchandise table. I thought about getting a concert shirt, but I wasn't about to dish out $30. What I was really hoping for was a used heroin syringe of Scott's, but they must have been all sold out.

By the time we left the Armory, it was 11:15pm and Shannon and I were beginning to get the midnight munchies. The only thing left to do was to get a cheeseburger trash plate with all the fixings from Empire Hots, up there in Webster, NY.

"Weird"

Any story wouldn't be complete without a Weird Al reference or cameo—but the hell with a that—this story is mostly about Weird Al!

Now I had never seen Weird Al before.

However, not only had Shannon seen Weird Al before, but she was a huge Weird AL fan and she met him!

It turned out that Weird Al was going to be in Buffalo, NY. He was playing a show at the Center for the Arts at the University at Buffalo on July 13, 2011.

On a whim, I asked my buddy Jason if he and his girlfriend Christina wanted to accompany us to the show. I knew Jason liked Weird Al, but I also knew he wasn't a huge fan of the concert scene. I told Jay that Weird Al was playing in the theater at UB and that there were assigned seats. I think that helped sway Jason's decision to a "Yes!"

On July 13th, Shannon and I tried to get out of work at 4:30pm so we could leave Rochester at a reasonable time.

Though the show wasn't starting until 7:30pm, Shannon and I were going to try to meet up with Jason and Christina for dinner at DiBella's Old Fashion Subs on Niagara Falls Boulevard.

I had to shoot home after work real quick. First, I had to let Teppo the dog out. Then I had to feed Teppo. Next, I had to poop and shower. After I got dressed, I grabbed the tickets and Shannon. Lastly we were off on the road, headed to DiBella's On Niagara Falls Boulevard!

We left Rochester a little after 5pm, which put us at DiBella's a little after 6:30pm.

Jason and Christina were not waiting that long for us.

I decided to be healthy and attempted a three cheese sub.

Shannon had a veggie sub and informed me that her sub was still healthier than mine. She said that though I got cheese on mine, that there was more calcium in the spinach that she got on her sub.

Jason had the Godfather and Christina had a turkey sub.

All four of us were obviously hungry because there was little conversation. Also, we had to eat quickly because we were pressed for time.

Once we were done with dinner, Shannon and I hopped into our 2003 Dodge Caravan while Jason and Christina hopped into Jason's Dodge pickup truck.

We caravanned it up Niagara Falls Boulevard to Maple Road. Then we hung a left off of Maple and onto Sweet Home Road. Within a mile, we were at UB North Campus and we found parking close enough to the Center for the Arts.

Of all the concerts I've been to, they never started on time. Weird Al was the only exception.

It was 7:30pm as the four of us entered the building where the venue was. As we got closer to the theater, we could hear that Weird Al was already playing!

Weird Al kicked off his set list with *Polka Face* off his latest album *Alpocalypse*, which was in support of the tour.

Shannon, Christina, Jason and I quickly found our seats in the middle of the balcony.

I did not recall any beer sales at the venue, probably because it was a college campus. It was not too big of a problem for Shannon and myself since we pregamed on the ride to DiBella's and the quick ride to UB.

Weird Al and his group then played *Frank's 2000" TV, TMZ, You Make Me,* and *You Don't Love Me Anymore*.

Then the stage went completely dark. There were screens that spanned across the top of the stage. These TVs turned on and started showing clips of Al TV. I remember watching the Al TV interviews years ago on MTV and VH-1. The TVs showed a couple Al TV interviews, like when Al "interviewed" Eminem, Avril Lavigne, and Celine Dion.

When the Al TV shorts were over, Weird Al and his band took the stage. The lights came on and there was Weird Al, dressed in his Kurt Cobain flannel and ripped up jeans! The band broke into *Smells Like Nirvana* and it was awesome! Weird Al re-enacted the *Smells Like Nirvana* music video, right down to gargling the water and spitting it out.

Once they finished *Smells Like Nirvana*, the stage lights went out and the TV monitors lit up again. This time, they played Weird Al television and movie references.

After the reference bit was over, Al and the band returned to the stage. Weird Al was dressed up as a Jungle Boat Captain from the Jungle Cruise ride at Disney. Weird Al performed *Skipper Dan*.

At the conclusion of *Skipper Dan*, the stage lights went out again and we got to watch more videos of Al TV.

Moments later, Weird Al and his band mates returned to the stage in normal clothes and played *Party in the CIA, Let Me Be Your Hog,* and *Canadian Idiot*.

It was around the time of *Canadian Idiot* that I had to break the seal. I was able to leave my seat, run down the stairs, find a bathroom (or "wash room" as Canadians called it), and pee, all while still hearing the song clear as day. I made it back to my seat before *Canadian Idiot* was over. *Canadian Idiot* was followed up by *Wanna B Ur Lovr*.

Next, Weird Al played a montage of quick melodies of some old classics including, *Money for Nothing/Beverly Hillbillies, My Bologna, Lasagna,* and *Eat It*. During *Eat It*, Weird Al wore his red Michael Jackson pleather jacket.

Again, the lights dimmed and the TV monitor lit up. In store for us was a smorgasbord of cameo clips of Weird Al in television and movies. Such cameos that were showcased were Weird Al on *The Simpsons,* Rob Zombie's *Halloween II,* and *The Naked Gun: From the Files of the Police Squad!,* just to name a few.

Soon after the cameo bit ended, the stage lights were turned on and Weird Al and his band were dressed up in their Amish garb, which only meant one thing, *Amish Paradise*!

Weird Al rocked out, or should I say, rapped out to *Amish Paradise* with his beard, plain black clothes, and hat.

After *Amish Paradise*, some more videos were shown on the screen because Al and his band needed some time to change their clothes again.

When Weird Al and his band came back out, the played two new songs off *Alpocalypse, Craigslist* and *Perform This Way*.

Yet again, the stage lights went out because Al and his band needed another wardrobe change.

After some more Weird Al footage on the screen, Weird Al came out in his gangsta clothes riding on his Segway dropping out the first couple verses to *White & Nerdy*! The whole place laughed and ate it up! On the screen above the stage, scenes from the *White*

& *Nerdy* music video were played, including the parts with Donnie Osmond!

At the conclusion of *White & Nerdy*, the stage lights went out, and we were privy to more Weird Al footage on the screens, but no one seemed to mind because all the Weird Al footage was hilarious!

The next footage that was shown on the TVs was the opening clip from Weird Al's *Fat* music video...*Yo! Ding Dong man! Ding Dong!Ding Dong, yo!* The rest of the music video played and suddenly a spot light shot on the stage. Weird Al had stormed out in the fat suit! It was awesome and the whole audience roared and clapped! Weird Al hit every note while acting out his music video. Everyone loved it! Especially when Santa came out on stage and fat Weird Al laid out Santa.

At the end of *Fat*, Weird Al announced his band mates by name and everyone clapped, cheered and gave a standing ovation.

Shannon was a little bummed out because they did not play her two most favorite Weird Al songs, the Star Wars parody songs.

Weird Al left the stage as his band members jammed on. Soon the band put down their instruments and left the stage.

However, the house lights did not go on...

Us fans started to cheer for an encore!

Minutes later, Weird Al, the band, and a couple extras came back on the stage!

The stage lights illuminated the stage again and every one was in Star Wars costumes! There was Darth Vader, Storm Troopers, Boba fett, R2-D2, and some other characters. Weird Al was dressed up as Obi-Wan. I am not a Star Wars nerd, so I didn't know the names of the other Star Wars characters that were on stage.

Weird Al started the encore with *The Saga Begins*. After the 15 minute long song, Weird Al ended his set with *Yoda*.

After *Yoda*, Weird Al and the band performed gibberish a cappella routine where they quoted different songs and catch phrases. They finished the a cappella routine with the last verse of *Yoda*.

And like that, the show was over.

It was around 10pm or so when we got out.

Jason asked us if we wanted to grab some drinks. Shannon and I told him, "Soytinly!"

The four of us caravanned it over to the recently opened Joe's Crab Shack.

There Jason, Shannon, and I enjoyed a couple beverages of the alcohol kind. Jason had a Molson, I had a Corona, and Shannon had Joe's Shark Attack drink. Christina drank a Pepsi.

We ordered some food at the bar. As we talked, Jason told us that he and Christina were going to get married. So we told them, "Congratulations!"

Jason said, "Yes! We're having a baby!"

Shannon and I unanimously said, "Oh! Congrats!"

Jason said, "Yeah! We're having twins!"

Shannon and I were happy for Jason and Christina.

Personally, I thought the day that Jay would get married would never come. I thought Jason was going to be a tomcat for life, but I suppose there are times when a man needs to settle down and get married.

It was well after midnight when Shannon and I got home to Rochester.

All four of us had fun at Weird Al and I would highly recommend to anyone to see him. He was a great performer and entertainer. I was a little bummed out that he did not play *Pretty Fly For a Rabbi, Jurassic Park,* or *Bedrock Anthem.* Oh well, maybe next time.

All-American

Part I

Friday, May 18, 2012, 4:30pm.

Shannon and her Nana were picking me up from work. The three of us were headed down to New Jersey for two reasons: first, we were bringing Nana back to her house in Toms River, NJ. Second—and the main reason—Shannon and I were going down to see the Foo Fighters at Bamboozle at Asbury Park.

Bamboozle Fest was a three day long rock fest at Asbury Park on the Jersey Shore. Each day had a different line up of bands. Friday had a whole bunch of no names. Saturday had the Foo Fighters as the headliner. Sunday night, Jersey's own Bon Jovi was the headliner; thankfully we weren't sticking around for that dog shit!

Initially, Shannon and I were excited about the concert because the Foo Fighters were headlining. Then we found out that Blink 182 and All American Rejects were also on the bill. We were thrilled to see the Foos again. I was quite excited to see Blink 182 because I had never seen them before. Shannon was extremely excited to see All American Rejects because they are one of her favorite bands. Plus she had never seen them live in concert before.

A week or two before the concert, Blink 182's drummer Travis Baker needed his tonsils removed so Blink 182 canceled all their shows for the entire month of May and into early June!

At first, I was pissed. I was really looking forward to seeing Blink. Then I heard that Blink 182 was being replaced by a special guest. I got a little excited hearing that because I thought they were going to get a cool band to cover for Blink.

I was beyond pissed off when I heard that My Chemical Romance was going to replace Blink 182!

Personally, I thought My Chemical Romance sucked. MCR was a shitty band and I didn't know how they had been on the music scene for so long. MCR needed to disappear, just like Good Charlotte finally disappeared!

Anyway, back to the road trip…

Shannon, Nana, and I left the Greater Rochester Area by 4:35pm. We hopped on the 90 and traveled east bound, towards Syracuse.

When we got to the Syracuse area, I decided to take I-690 south because it was a short cut to pick up I-81 south.

As we approached downtown Syracuse, Nana and I both saw caution signs redirecting traffic. The sign said that there was heavy traffic congestion and construction ahead and to take Exit 12 to get to I-81 south.

As I followed the detour signs, I think someone was playing a trick on us out of towners. Moments later, the detour signs were gone and we were in the ghetto.

While driving through the ghetto, stop signs soon became stoptionals. Traffic lights were just a mere four way stop.

During our tour through the ghetto, the three of us noticed a strong odor. I wasn't sure if a part of the city smelled like some skunk weed or if an actual skunk had sprayed its scent. I didn't think that skunks lived in the city, so I thought that there was a Rastafarian party going on or Snoop Dog was in the area.

After our 15 minute tour of Syracuse we found our way to I-81 and we were back on course.

About an hour south of Syracuse was Binghamton.

Binghamton, NY was now my new pit stop town because they had Sonic, America's Drive In! At the time, it was the only Sonic in New York.

I ordered a Philly Steak and Cheese sub with tots and a root beer. The steak and cheese sub was great. The tots were nice and salty; like little mini salt licks! And the root beer was good. I like getting draft root beer off the tap, because it tastes better than bottled root beer.

Shannon ordered a Chicago Hot Dog with tots and a coke with chocolate syrup. Shannon enjoyed her dog and tots, but not her chocolate flavored coke.

Nana had a cheeseburger with tots and a milk shake.

I asked Nana, "Hey, what kind of shake did you get?"

Nana looked at me like I was a doofus and said, "Chocolate! Is there any other kind?!"

I thought about it briefly and said, "Well, no…I would agree."

After dinner, we were back on the road again.

We finally arrived at Nana's house around 11pm. We were all exhausted, so after we unpacked the 2003 Dodge shaggin wagon, we all went to bed.

Saturday May 19th was finally here. Shannon was ecstatic to finally see the All American Rejects and the Foo Fighters. I was excited to see the Foo Fighters for the 8th time!

We were showered, dressed, and ready for the show by 9am.

Nana, Shannon, and I picked up some bagels because we were going over to Shannon's Aunt Carol's for breakfast (Carol was one of Nana's daughters).

We had breakfast with Aunt Carol and Uncle Steve and their three kids; Jayson, Katlyn, and Tyler.

Jayson agreed to drive us to the concert because Shannon and I had no idea where we were going.

He had bought tickets for the entire Bamboozle Fest; Friday, Saturday, and Sunday.

Shannon asked him what time we should leave for the show.

Jayson said, "Oh it's only in Asbury Park. It's not that far away. We probably have to drive on the Parkway for about an hour, and then we have to drive to a parking lot and take a 30 minute shuttle to the venue. Then you have to go through security..."

"Jayson" I interrupted, "How long does it take to get there and what time do we have to leave?"

Jayson said, "Oh it will take about two hours to get there. Doors open around noon or 1pm. As long as we leave by noon, we should be good."

Uncle Steve interrupted Jayson, "You are not going anywhere until you mow our lawn and the neighbor's lawn!"

Jayson whined back to his dad, "Come on dad! But but but...I I I..."

Uncle Steve said, "Jayson! I don't want to hear it! You've had all week to mow the lawns and you've procrastinated and put it off. You're not going to the show if you don't finish your jobs!"

"But dad!" Jayson whined back to Uncle Steve.

Shannon told Jayson, "All I really want is to see the All American Rejects and I don't want to miss them."

Jayson said, "Oh don't worry. They go on at like 4 or something. So we'll have plenty of time."

Uncle Steve told Jayson several times to get his ass in gear and to mow the lawns. Jayson just ignored Uncle Steve and came up with different excuses why he couldn't.

I finally asked, "Well, how big is the neighbor's lawn?"

Uncle Steve said, "It's the one across the street."

I looked outside the window and saw a house with a small yard. I asked Uncle Steve and Jayson, "Hey! Is it that house across the street with the small yard?"

Both simultaneously said, "Yes."

I said, "I'm failing to see the dilemma here. It would only take you an hour to push mow that."

Uncle Steve said, "Oh Jayson doesn't push mow their lawn. He has a ride on lawn mower."

I looked right at Jayson who was sitting on his butt. "Dude!" I shouted.

Jayson looked up at me through his Justin Bieber haircut and said, "Wud?"

I said, "You gotta be f-ing kidding me! All you have to do is cut the grass with a ride on mower and you are complaining about that? Quit dicking around and get off your lazy butt and mow the damn lawn!"

Jayson said, "Uh, well. I need help getting the mower out of the shed."

I looked at Jayson and said, "You gotta be kidding me…fine! Come on, get up!"

So I helped Jayson get the ride on mower out of the shed. It was close to 11am before Jayson finally started his chores.

Shannon and I waited in the family room for what felt like an hour. We finally heard the lawn mower across the street stop. Moments later, Jayson came in the house.

"Uh, Adam" Jayson said.

"Duh, Jayson" I replied.

"Uh, I got the mower stuck in the mud, can you help me?" Jayson inquired.

I said, "Yup."

Jayson had gotten the mower stuck in about two inches of mud. It took a couple minutes, but we were able to free the mower.

In the meantime, I had Uncle Steve show me his new baby, a red 1985 Chevrolet Corvette, with stick shift! Uncle Steve had picked the car up for cheap but it needed some body work and minor interior work. He added that if I liked the C4, I should avoid the first year of the new model, 1984, because they had Crossfire injection. Crossfire injection was a brilliant, problematic headache that GM designed. For the 1985 model year Corvettes, Chevy scrapped the Crossfire for the more reliable tuned port fuel injection. Uncle Steve said that his Vette also had the "4+3 transmission." The transmission was a 4 speed manual with an automatic over drive with the top three gears. Somehow it helped the car pass government emission standards.

Uncle Steve decided to give Nana a ride in the Vette. Nana didn't want her hair messed up, so Uncle Steve had to put the Targa Top back in.

With Nana in the car, Uncle Steve backed the car out of the driveway and onto their quiet side street. Next Uncle Steve dumped the clutch and smoked the tires! As the car stood still, burnt rubber smoke billowed out from behind the Corvette. Shannon and I heard Nana swear at Uncle Steve, "Holy shit! What are you doing Steve?!"

Right then, the rear end got traction and launched the car off like a rocket!

It was close to 1pm when Jayson finally got done with the lawns.

Shannon and I were getting increasingly antsy. Shannon and I didn't pay $80 a ticket so we could miss half of the festival.

Jayson soon procrastinated hopping into the shower.

I asked Jay, "What the hells the holdup bro? Just hop in the shower or I'll just break out the power washer."

In the meantime, Jayson's girlfriend Bre and her friend must have changed outfits five times.

Once Jayson was finally done with his shower, he just walked around the house with a towel on.

I looked at Jayson and asked, "Why are you walking around with a towel on!? Why don't you get dressed so we can go to the show?"

Jay answered, "Well Bre and her friend are in my room. They are doing their make up or changing or something."

I snapped, "Jay! Go in your room, get your clothes, and change in your sisters' room!"

15 minutes later, Jayson was dressed.

Then Jayson had to blow dry his hair. By that point in time, Shannon and I were already upset with Jayson. "Jayson!" I yelled. "No one cares about your Justin Bieber hair! Can we just get in the car and go?!"

"Well I gotta do my hair!" Jayson whined back.

I said, "Why do you have to do your hair? Who are you trying to impress? You already have a girlfriend." I looked at Bre and asked her, "Bre, do you like Jayson's hair?"

Bre giggled and said, "Yes."

"Fine! See Jayson, your hair is perfectly fine. Let's go. There's going to be 1000's of people there and they don't care about your hair."

It was well after 2pm by the time we left Aunt Carol's house. I had Bre stop off at a liquor store so that I could buy beer and some airplane sized bottles of booze. Moments later, we pulled onto the New Jersey Parkway.

Bre was driving the five of us in her hooptie Scion. Bre put the pedal to the metal as we hit 85 mph down the Parkway. The Parkway was surprisingly smooth sailing; there was no traffic. It only took us about 40 minutes to drive from Toms River to Route 36.

Once we pulled onto Route 36, we became a part of the four lane grid lock parking lot. It took us literally over an hour to drive three miles to Monmouth Park Racetrack.

We parked in the racetrack's parking lot. Then we needed to walk across the mammoth parking lot to catch a motor coach to Assberry Park. During the walk over to the buses, Shannon and I downed a few cans of Miller Lite.

Once we got to where the buses were, we had to wait in a massively long line. As we waited a half hour in line, Shannon and I kicked back some more Millers.

Eventually it became time to board the bus. This was around the time when Shannon and I got separated from Jayson, Bre, and the friend. Shannon and I got the last two seats on the bus to Assberry Park.

Shannon and I now had a 30 minute bus ride ahead of us. We killed the time by drinking some more Miller Lites.

The ride through town to Assberry Park was a nice one. There were a lot of fancy looking mansions.

As we were riding to our destination, Shannon started to tear up. She hissed to me, "It's already 4:30! By the time we get to the venue, it's gonna be practically 5! I'm missing All American Rejects! That was the only thing I wanted to see and Jayson fucked it up because he's a lazy ass!"

The bus finally dropped us off by the beach. The bus conductor gave us vouchers to get back on the bus for after the concert. The conductor said, "These tickets are to re-board the bus! You must have them to return to Monmouth Park Racetrack. Make sure to come back here to pick up the bus. We are at Asbury and Kingsley."

Shannon and I grabbed our vouchers and took off to the boardwalk.

We had no paper tickets for the festival, but rather wrist bands that had a scan-able computer chip in them.

We made it through security and found our way to the main stage. Unfortunately there were no bands performing on the main stage; it was just the roadies doing a set change. I looked at Shannon and said, "Well maybe they are setting up for All American Rejects? You know these concerts never start on time and they always run late…"

Shannon asked the girl standing next to us, "Excuse me, did All American Rejects just play or are they setting up for them?"

The girl said, "They just played. You missed them by 20 minutes…"

Shannon said, "Thanks." Shannon turned around to me and said, "Fuck…fuck! Fuckfuckfuckfuckfuckfuck!!"

We were right next to a beer tent, so I said, "Let me grab you a beer, it will hopefully take the edge off."

The only beer at the beer tent was Coors Light…Shannon would have needed a lot of Coors Light to take the edge off.

Once we got our brews we made our way down to the beach.

In the meantime, I had texted one of our friends, Teri. I wanted to know where All American Rejects were playing next. I wasn't sure if they were playing locally and we could catch them.

A few minutes later, Teri got back to me. Teri said that All American was playing a few more shows, but then taking off for Europe for a summer long tour. Shannon was bummed out.

On the bright side, the concert venue was different and interesting. I had to say that I have never been to a rock concert that was on a boardwalk and beach, overlooking the Atlantic Ocean. Concert goers were able to walk the beach, but we couldn't go into the ocean because it was fenced off. There were a few people in fishing boats, catching the show for free.

While we waited for the Foos to take the stage, there were a few bands that we listened to as back ground noise.

Jimmy Eat World took the stage after All American Rejects. I never got into Jimmy Eat World. I only knew their two radio hits. Jimmy Eat World started off their hour long set with *Sweetness*, which was the only song I recognized of theirs that afternoon.

Less Than Jake was playing at a side stage. I never got into Less Than Jake, but I remembered that they always played at the Vans Warped Tour that came to Darien Lake.

Motion City Soundtrack, Anti-Flag, and Boy Sets Fire were also on the bill, but I didn't really care about seeing them.

In the meantime, Shannon's phone was dying. Shannon shot off a quick text to Jayson, telling him that her phone was about to shut off and that we would try to meet them at the car after the show...

Once Jimmy Eat World finished their set, the roadies came out and swapped all the equipment for My Chemical Romance. MCR came out on stage and I went to the port-o-potty to piss out a few beers. MCR played for one long painful hour. Shannon and I were so relieved when My Chemical Romance finally left the stage! All we needed to do was to wait for the set change and then it would be Foo Fighting time!

Soon it was the moment Shannon and I had been waiting for! It was still daylight as the Foos took the main stage and the fans screamed and cheered!

The Foos kicked off their set with one of their great songs, *All My Life*.

The Foo Fighters were still touring in support of their latest record, *Wasting Light*, so it was no surprise that they played new song *Rope*.

Next the Foo Fighters played *The Pretender* and *My Hero*.

In between songs, front man Dave Grohl yelled out to us, "Hey! Hey! Hey! Hey! Hey! How the fuck are you?!" Dave went on to tell us that they were going to play for a really long time.

As the Foo Fighters played *Learn to Fly* (one of my other favorite Foos songs) the ocean breeze began to smell like some skunk weed.

Other songs off the new album the Foos played were *White Limo* and *Arlandria*.

Fans and the Foo Fighters were jamming out to *Breakout* when I realized that I had the backpack which contained the airplane bottles of booze, so I grabbed one. I pulled out a warm root beer flavored vodka bottle. The warm vodka tasted disgusting and burned. I didn't like it so I gave it to Shannon. I was still thirsty, so I grabbed another bottle. This time I came up with cotton candy flavored vodka. The cotton candy was warm and burned, but it tasted better than the root beer.

Before playing *Cold Day in the Sun*, front man Dave Grohl switched places with drummer Taylor Hawkins. Taylor sang lead vocals for *Cold Day in the Sun* as Dave banged on the drums.

Next the Foos played *Big Me*, and yet again, I forgot to bring Mentos to throw at the stage. Instead I grabbed another airplane sized bottle of vodka, popped open the top, and tossed it down the hatch! After a few warm vodkas, they stopped burning.

Big Me was followed by another new cut, *Walk*, then another, *These Days*. But during the song, the Foos teased us fans by playing the opening notes and melody to *Times Like These* before finishing *These Days*.

The Foos kicked it old school and played a couple goodies off of their second album *The Colour and the Shape*. Until that show, I had never heard the Foos play in concert *Hey, Johnny Park!* They also played *Monkey Wrench*, which is one of my favorite songs.

Before playing *Monkey Wrench* Dave talked to us and thanked us for coming to the show. He said it meant a lot to him and he was excited to see little Foos fans that were influenced by him and recently picked up a guitar so they could be in a huge rock band like the Foos. Dave encouraged them to do it and chase their dream. He also dedicated *Monkey Wrench* to "all the fucking rock and rollers!"

During *Monkey Wrench* there were a lot of crowd surfers that floated on by…Actually, come to think of it, there were crowd surfers pretty much all throughout the Foos concert! Dave added to the excitement by running back and forth across the stage, jamming on his guitar and hyping up the fans!

Midway through *Monkey Wrench*, with an upside down guitar, Dave spent a few minutes ripping out a few blues riffs, notes and melodies. Dave went so far as to laying down on the stage and playing the guitar, much to the fans amusement and enjoyment.

I was thrilled when I heard Dave tell us that everything started with the next song…*This Is a Call*.

Normally I liked it when bands did covers. That night the Foos covered Pink Floyd's *In the Flesh?* and Tom Petty and the Heartbreakers' *Breakdown*. I had a few singles and B-sides of the Foos that contained cover songs that I would have preferred to hear, like Gerry Rafferty's *Baker Street*, Prince's *Darling Nikki,* or Paul McCartney and Wings' *Band on the Run*. If the Foos wanted to cover Pink Floyd, I would have rather of heard *Have a Cigar*. Last year when Shannon and I saw the Foos in Buffalo, they played *In the Flesh?* and *Breakdown*, so I would have welcomed any other cover tunes.

The Foos redeemed themselves by playing *Best of You*. *Best of You* was an obvious fan favorite, especially considering the fact that all the fans sang along, word for word!

Lastly, Dave told us that they had to get going soon because they needed to be in New York City in a few minutes because they were a part of the musical act that evening on Saturday Night Live. Mick Jagger (of the Rolling Stones) was hosting SNL and was the musical act, with the Foo Fighters as the backup band.

The Foo Fighters ended the evening with *Everlong*.

After the Foos finished their set, they left the stage, bound for the chopper to take them to NYC. By that time, it was already night time and Shannon and I had the munchies, so we went in search of food.

We stumbled upon a food vender on the boardwalk. Shannon and I both had a steak and cheese sub and a huge tub of boardwalk fries.

After we finished our late dinner, I noticed there was no fence blocking me from going into the ocean. I wanted my beach and ocean fix so I hopped off the boardwalk and ran down the beach, and into the ocean.

The ocean was freezing! I instantly ran back to land.

Shannon and I then wandered around the boardwalk for a bit before we realized that we needed to get back to the bus to get us to the car; this became our next dilemma. First of all, we had no idea where we were. We had never been to Assberry Park. Secondly, everything looked different in the dark.

Shannon and I wandered off the boardwalk and back towards the mainland. We walked a couple blocks before we started seeing coach buses, similar to the one that took us to the venue.

We soon came upon the location to where the bus had originally dropped us off. However, we could not find where the buses were picking up the concert goers.

Right across the street from where we were standing was a bar with a bouncer. I figured I'd ask the bouncer for directions since he must have known the area.

I looked both ways before Shannon and I crossed the street.

I approached the bouncer and said, "Hey bud, I have a real quick question for you."

The fist pumping douche bag bouncer said, "Yea, no problem. I just need to see your ID first."

I said, "Yea, no problem. Here you go" as I gave him my ID. As the fist pumping douche bag bouncer looked at my ID I asked him, "Hey, so we just left the concert and we need to catch one of those buses. Do you know where we can catch one of those buses?"

The first pumping douche bag said, "Yea, at a bus stop, huh huh! It's a $10 cover charge."

I looked at him and said, "I'm not paying to go into you shitty douche bag bar..." As Shannon and I walked away, I thought the HGH, roid raged, fist pumping douche bag bouncer was going to pound the crap out of me, but he didn't. He probably glared me down and popped his collar.

Shannon and I soon saw a cop directing traffic.

I approached the cop and said, "Excuse me officer, I have a really quick question for you."

The cop continued to direct traffic and said, "Shoot."

I said, "We just left the concert and we have no idea where to catch the bus back to the parking lot."

The cop said, "If you're going back to the Monmouth Park Racetrack parking lot, go down this road 'til it ends, hang a left, and they are boarding the buses there."

I thanked the cop and Shannon and I were soon on our merry way.

Shannon and I walked down the road and took the left turn as directed. As we made the left hand turn, we could see a line of buses and a line of people that looked to be a half mile long!

Shannon and I hopped in line to wait for our bus.

We were in line for at least a half hour before Shannon noticed that Jayson, Bre, and their friend were a few people in front of us.

The five of us ended up waiting in line for close to an hour and a half to just board the bus. Then we had a half hour ride back to the parking lot. Once we got to the parking lot, we still had at least another 45 minute car ride back to Jayson's house.

By the time Shannon and I got back to Nana's house, it was already well past 1:30am. That was one long day!

Sunday morning greeted me with heat stroke or heat exhaustion; *it definitely was not a hangover.* I think the reason why I wasn't feeling well was because I was dehydrated from the sun and heat. I had minor sun burns and did not eat much the day before.

Shannon and I showered and got ready to go back out to Aunt Carols to figure out lunch plans.

Aunt Carol, Uncle Steve, Katlyn, Tyler, Nana, Shannon, and I ended up having pizza at the Anchor Inn in Ocean Gate, N.J. Jayson didn't join us for pizza because he was still sleeping.

After lunch, Shannon and I said our good byes to the family.

On our ride back home, Shannon and I made a quick pit stop in Hope, NJ. For years, every time I went down to Jersey with Shannon, I always saw a road sign for the Land of Make Believe. For years I always wondered what the Land of Make Believe was, but that day I finally had my question answered!

The Land of Make Believe was a seasonal water and amusement park.

By the time Shannon and I reached Binghamton, NY, my head trauma was gone and I had to pee. Also, since we were in Binghamton, we needed to stop at Sonic again. Shannon had another Chicago Dog and I tried a bacon cheeseburger. I have to say, after that visit, I was a little Sonic-ed out…I think it may have been the beginning of the end of my Sonic love affair. Even though the food tasted good, I always wound up with a massive stomach ache!

Hours later, Shannon and I finally arrived home.

Since we never got to see the Foo Fighters and Mick Jagger on SNL, I uploaded their clip on the internet. Mick and the Foos played Rolling Stones song *19th Nervous Breakdown* and *It's Only Rock 'n Roll (But I Like It)*. Mick sang lead vocals with Dave on backup vocals. It was an interesting performance, *but I liked it*.

Part II

A few months had passed since our trip to New Jersey.

I was bored one night and was trolling the internet. On a whim, I decided to look up the All American Rejects' website. I was interested in when they were playing State side again.

To my surprise, All American Rejects were playing shows back in the States as of August. There were two dates that stuck out to me. On Sunday September 16th, the All American Rejects were playing in Utica, New York. Utica was home to Utica Club beer, the 1st legal brewery after Prohibition. Also, Utica was about two and a half hours away from Rochester. The other date that caught my eye was the following weekend, Saturday September 22nd in Boston.

I initially thought about surprising Shannon about the show, but I did not know which show to take her to, so I weighed it out.

On the one hand, Utica was close to home. Plus, if we went to Utica, we could have toured the FX Matt Brewery, where Utica Club and Saranac beer are brewed. The only down side was that the show was on a Sunday night. We would have either needed to have taken the Monday off from work and gotten a hotel room for the night or driven home after the concert.

The other option was to go to Boston for a Saturday night show. If we went to Boston, then I could take Shannon to the Sam Adams Brewery again, and hopefully this time she could enjoy it! The last time Shannon and I were in Boston, I took Shannon to the brewery, but she fell ill with gallstones. As a direct result, she missed the beer tour. Packed into that same weekend as the beer tour, we were supposed to go whale watching. However, whale watching canceled on us because the waters were too choppy.

Instead the whale watching company, Boston Harbor Cruises, gave us a lifetime rain check…So I think my decision was made!

It was an early August evening when I called Shannon and told her to request the weekend of September 22nd off. Shannon asked me why she needed to request that weekend off.

I did not want to burst the surprise, so I held my ground and told her, "I have a surprise for you and I don't want to burst the surprise. I'm holding my ground."

Shannon said, "Okay, but can you give me a hint?"

I replied, "Yes! Here's your hint…*I hope we do it!*"

I could tell Shannon rolled her eyes before saying, "Ugh…What stupid thing do you want to do this time?"

I quickly back pedaled and said, "Duh, *I hope we do it* after the rock concert!"

Shannon's curiosity was quipped, "Ooo! Who's playing?"

I knew that if I wanted to get some, I had to crack and spill my guts. So I blurted out, "All American Rejects are playing in Boston that weekend and if we go, then we can go on the Sam Adams beer tour and attempt to go whale watching again!" And ladies and gentlemen, the rest is what I would call history!

Tickets and hotel were booked soon afterwards.

Eventually it was time for our big weekend!

I got home from work around 5pm. I had to poop and shower. After the shower I had to get dressed. Once I got dressed, I had to pack my bag and then the van. I made sure that we had everything ready and planned for the trip…

I had MapQuest driving directions from our house to the hotel. I had directions from the hotel to Sam Adams Brewery. I had directions from Sam Adams Brewery to Boston Harbor Cruises. I had directions from Boston Harbor Cruises to House of Blues. I had directions from House of Blues to the hotel. I had all my ends covered, we were golden!

Shannon and I were finally on the road by 7pm. By my calculations, we were going to arrive at the Crown Plaza by 1:30am.

Shannon and I kicked off our venture by traveling in our 2003 Dodge Caravan. Our minivan already had 180,000+ on the odometer. The night before the trip, I wined and dined my baby. I gave her an oil change, new spark plugs, and wires. I made sure to give her a nice lube job and I topped off all her fluids.

I drove until we hit Massachusetts. I found a rest stop and told Shannon, "I gotta pee and I'm falling asleep."

Shannon said, "Ok, that's fine. I'm still on the overnights schedule from work, so I'm wide awake."

After I peed, I rode shot gun while Shannon drove the last leg of the journey.

I'm not gonna lie, but even though I was dead ass tired, I could not sleep a wink. I was scared and nervous to let Shannon drive alone because I figured that she needed an awake and alert co-pilot. Even though she said she was awake and coherent, I still wanted to provide her with company.

During the drive, Shannon played a couple of the Rejects' CDs to prime me for their concert because I only knew a couple songs from the Rejects.

Shannon and I were staying at the Crown Plaza in Newton. The Crown Plaza was built on top of the 90…wait, sorry, the Mass Turnpike…They don't call it the 90 anymore when you hit Massachusetts.

Even though we had MapQuest directions, we thought the hotel would be fairly easy to find, since we could see it on top of the highway. Well, we were wrong about that.

When we pulled off the highway, it was roughly 1:30am, dark, and rainy. The exit ramp dumped us off onto a four lane road. Each road spider webbed off into two other roads. It was difficult to find which road we needed because for some stupid reason, Boston lacked street signs and/or hid them behind foliage.

Needless to say, we got lost trying to find the hotel that was right in front of us because of the damn roads.

Shannon and I eventually found the hotel and the adjacent parking garage. Once we parked the minivan, we lugged our bags into the lobby.

The night shift receptionist's name was Charles, and he seemed like an odd chap. Chuck was wearing a three piece suit; I think it may have been polyester. He was wearing a pin that read, "Bobby Kennedy for President." I think the suit and the pin were from the same vintage. Charles had a weird and obscure personality.

As Shannon and I were checking in, I couldn't help feeling as if we were in an episode of the Twilight Zone.

Charles spoke with that unflattering Boston accent…*Basstin!*

Chuck told us that the Crown Plaza had a complimentary breakfast in the morning and then he gave us our room keys.

Shannon and I were staying on the 3rd Floor.

In short order, Shannon and I found our room, but our keys did not work. Shannon went down to see our boy Chuck again to get the key situation ironed out while I waited in front of our room with the bags.

Moments later, Shannon returned with Chuck. Chuck mentioned that they had been having problems with the new machine programing the room keys. Chuck used his master key to let us into the room. Chuck reassured us that if there was anything we needed, to just give him a buzz.

Once Shannon and I were safely in the room, I locked the dead bolt and put the chair up underneath the door handle.

Next, I turned on the idiot box and fell asleep to some background noise.

Saturday morning came quicker than expected.

Shannon and I needed to be out the door by 9am so we could make it to the Sam Adams brewery for the 10am beer tour.

Shannon and I were up by 8:40am. We were showered and out of the room shortly after 9am.

Shannon wanted to grab some food real quick before we left for the brewery. She figured that it would probably be a good idea to have food in her stomach before drinking a lot of beer.

So we walked down to the breakfast area so she could grab a bagel.

In the meantime, I ran to the car to drop some stuff off.

Once I met back up with Shannon, I asked her if she was ready. She told me that she was just waiting for her bagel to finish being toasted. She said that if I wanted a coffee, to grab one.

I looked around the joint to try to find a to-go cup, but all I saw were coffee mugs. As I looked around the breakfast area, I noticed that all the tables were set for dining; place mats, utensils, cloth napkins, coffee mugs, etc. I took a quick look at the continental buffet breakfast and everything looked disgusting, from the dried up eggs to the funky street meat that was supposed to resemble sausage and bacon. After surveying the landscape, I nudged Shannon and said, "Let's go."

Shannon said, "Yea, but we have to wait for my bagel."

I said, "Just leave it. I don't think your bagel is continental or complimentary."

"Yea, but the guy last night told us about the continental breakfast," Shannon replied.

I said, "Yea, but there are not disposable plates or garbage cans for your waste. Also, there are no to-go coffee cups..."

Just then a waiter came up to us and asked us if we were ok.

I told him that we were fine.

At that moment in time, Shannon was buttering her bagel. The waiter asked, "Would you like me to ring that up?"

Shannon's lousy, stale bagel cost $4.50! All I thought was, "You gotta be *freaking* kidding me!"

So needless to say, we were late leaving the hotel.

According to MapQuest, the Sam Adams brewery was only 6 miles away from the hotel, or 23 minutes away from the hotel.

That damn "continental non-continental" bagel put us behind the 8 ball; we did not leave Crown Plaza until after 9:30am for our 10am beer tour.

Shannon and I normally had great luck with MapQuest and never get lost. But Boston appeared to be the Bermuda Triangle for MapQuest. Sadly, we got lost trying to find the brewery.

It seemed like every other street in Boston had the same name.

It seemed like there were no street signs in Boston.

It seemed like if there were street signs, they were hidden behind a tree in Boston.

It seemed like if there was a road sign, the lettering was faded so you couldn't tell what fucking road you were on or wanted to turn on.

Long story short, we got lost but somehow found the brewery by 10am. Unfortunately we couldn't find a spot to park and every other road was a one way.

I looked at Shannon and said, "The hell with it. Let's just find out where this Boston Harbor Cruise thing sets sail from. Our whale watching trip leaves at 12:30pm. The next beer tour is at 11am and it lasts an hour. I don't think we will be able to do both, and we came here primarily for the whale watching."

Shannon agreed.

I printed out MapQuest directions from Sam Adams to Boston Harbor Cruises and yet again, we got lost trying to drive the 10 or so miles to get to the harbor!

One might ask why we didn't use a GPS. Well the answer was quite simple. I liked to shun modern technology. Shannon and I both thought that GPS sucked. We have tried several varieties and they all have gotten us lost, and told us we were on a road that didn't exist.

Shannon and I found ourselves lost in the middle of downtown Boston.

We were stuck at a red light when I asked Shannon to ask a couple of cops where we were and how to get to the harbor.

The cops were quite nice and said, "Oh take a right at the light, go all the way down, hang a left, and it will be a few blocks down on your right."

I do have to say that even though it sucked getting lost in Boston, the scenery was quite nice. Boston had a lot of nice buildings and neighborhoods. Everything was clean and I liked the idea that people actually used the mass transit systems.

By the time we parked the van and found Boston Harbor Cruises, it was around 11am. Shannon and I checked in and got our tickets for our 12:30pm whale watching tour.

Since Shannon and I had an hour and a half to kill, we decided to walk around the area a little.

I remembered the last time I was on a boat that I got sick. I also remembered Grandpa Ziggy told me that when he was in the German Navy, that the sailors received chocolate to settle their sea sick stomachs.

There was a convenient store close by, so Shannon and I stopped in real quick. I bought a couple Hershey bars. As we were cashing out, I noticed the store had hard liquor behind the counter. I saw that they had a small bottle of chocolate toffee, so I picked that up as well.

Next, we walked a few stores down to Dunkin Donuts, where Shannon and I grabbed some hot chocolate.

Then we walked back to the pier and parked it on a bench that was right next to our whale watching boat.

Shannon and I ate one of the candy bars and we spiked one of the hot chocolates. The liquor tasted awful, and Shannon reminded me, "What did you expect for a $6 bottle of booze?"

Shannon and I enjoyed our hour of people watching.

Soon it was time to board the boat.

But first, we had to wait in line and get our stupid picture taken. Once we gave the ticket collector our tickets, then we were allowed to board.

Shannon and I walked up to the top deck. Minutes later, our boat sounded its horn and we exited the harbor.

As soon as we exited the harbor, our boat captain floored the boat. Shannon and I had to hold onto to the railing for dear life and it was awesome!

After a few minutes, some crew members came up on deck and told all the patrons that the seas were too rough and that we needed to get below deck. That was easier said than done. There were at least 15 of us that struggled to make our way to the stairs of the main deck. The boat was going so fast and hitting so many waves, that it made it virtually impossible to walk, especially down the stairs.

It took a while for Shannon and me to make it down to the main deck. We found an open booth in the galley. As soon as I sat down, the sea sickness hit me! I instantly turned green and wanted to vomit!

About 20 minutes later, we arrived at the tip of Cape Cod. Our boat captain stopped the boat so we could look at whales. All the tourists flocked out of the galley and to the perimeter of the boat to catch a glimpse of whales. I was still trying to catch my stomach, so I stayed back.

Shannon finally had to drag me out of the booth and onto the deck so that we could see the whales, and whale watching we did. There were tons of whales, all swimming pretty close to the boat, shooting water out of their blow holes. Then they would submerge back under water and flick their tails before going fully under water.

Whale watching lasted close to an hour.

The trip back to the harbor made me sea sick again.

I was beyond green by the time we got back to land.

After exiting the boat, I had to sit on a park bench for a few minutes to get my color and stomach back.

Once I was feeling better, Shannon and I devised a game plan. It was midafternoon and we decided to just head to the House of Blues.

Even though the House of Blues was only a few miles away from downtown, it was a nightmare and took forever to drive to the concert venue.

As we circumnavigated our way through downtown Boston, we found ourselves going the wrong way down a one way every other block. And it didn't help matters that we constantly got stuck in a bicycle race!

Eventually we made it to the general area of the House of Blues. We found parking right next to Fenway Park.

After parking the van, we walked the block or so to the House of Blues. During our walk to the venue, a wonderful thing happened. The Boston Red Sux had lost and all the fans were walking with their tails between their legs!

Shannon and I were early for the show at the House of Blues and there was already a line of concert goers that wrapped around the building. Shannon saw the huge line and got nervous that we would not get into the venue on time and miss the All American Rejects for the second time.

Shannon found an employee and found out that the All American Rejects we not the headliner that night. Boys Like Girls, who was the opening act on the tour, was the headlining act that evening because they were from Boston. With that being said, Shannon and I had more than an hour to kill before the All American Rejects took the stage.

By then, I had recovered my stomach and color. Shannon and I were both hungry, so we decided to have a late lunch at the House of Blues. Shannon had some sort of salad and I had adult mac and cheese. We both washed our food down with beer.

After dinner, we ordered another round of beer, which we were allowed to take into the venue.

The restaurant was connected to it, so after getting our tickets scanned, we entered the venue.

At first, the venue looked like Queen Moussette's mansion from *Blue Brothers 2000*. It was an interesting looking place. The concert hall was multilevel. The main floor, where our tickets were good for, was standing room only general admission.

The second level had a perimeter standing room only section. There were a couple boxed suites that had couches and such.

The third level had balcony theater seating.

While we waited for the All American Rejects to take the stage, I went to the bar to grab some beer. I was surprised that there was no line for the beer.

When I got back to Shannon with the beer, I mentioned that there was nobody at the bar.

We surveyed the joint and noticed that we were the oldest people who weren't chaperoning kids.

Soon it was the moment that Shannon was waiting for!

The lights went out and fans started to cheer. Suddenly Carl Orff's *O Fortuna* rang out through the speakers. A short while later, the All American Rejects took the stage and opened with a song I knew, *Dirty Little Secret*. Since I wasn't a huge Rejects buff, I had to ask Shannon what songs the All American Rejects played.

Lead singer Tyson Ritter had a bushy hair do with a black shirt and black and white striped pants. The black and white striped pants gave off a real Beetlejuice effect.

The Rejects played *It Ends Tonight, Heartbeat Slowing Down, Move Along Kids in the Street, My Paper Heart*, and a couple other songs that I didn't know.

The band played their song *Mona Lisa* while lead singer Tyson Ritter got the bright idea to climb up on one of the speakers that was on the stage. From the speaker, he climbed up to the second floor. He then walked around on the outside of the balcony, hanging onto the railing. I thought he was going to jump—but alas, he did not.

The Rejects ended their set with another song I knew, *Gives You Hell*.

Boston's own Boys Like Girls took the stage. I wasn't a fan of Boys Like Girls, but all the teeny bopper girls loved them. I thought Boys Like Girls should have changed their name to 20-Something Year Old Boys Like Under Aged Girls.

During the band's set, they told all the teeny boppers to call the radio station after the show and tell them how great they were. Shannon was understandably outraged, "That's bull shit! They should let their music and their performance do the speaking for them! They shouldn't have to tell people how "great" they are!"

The best part about Boys Like Girls was when they finally finished their set. It meant that Shannon and I could finally meet the All American Rejects!

Oh yeah, did I forget to tell you that I paid a little extra money and surprised Shannon with special meet and greet tickets?!

As soon as the show ended, Shannon and I went up to the second floor and waited in line for our meet and greet session. There were at least 75 people in line to meet All American Rejects, and naturally Shannon and I were towards the back of the line. As we waited in line, House of Blues crew members cleaned up the venue because they had another event that night—a drag show. In 45 minutes, the cleaning crew was able to clean the main floor of empty beer cans and put couches, tables, and chairs on the floor. On the stage, a DJ was doing sound checks.

Each band member said "hi" to Shannon and me. I told them they put on a good show. One of the band members had his bull dog puppy with him. Shannon and I got our picture taken with the band and we each got an autographed poster.

Since all the fun was over, Shannon and I drove back to the hotel.

The following morning, Shannon and I walked around town, trying to find breakfast at a diner, but we didn't find any such establishment that was open in our neck of the woods. We ended up settling on Dunkin Donuts.

After breakfast, I attempted to get us back on the 90 but ended up driving parallel with the 90 for miles until we finally found an entrance ramp for the 90 westbound.

As soon as we crossed over into New York I was able to find the Buffalo Bills game on the radio! During the entire drive across the state, I listened to John Murphy call the Bills game. Buffalo ended up beating the Browns in Cleveland 24-14!

Part III

Even before Blink 182 canceled their Bamboozle show, I wanted to see them in concert. In the following months and years after the Bamboozle show, I checked the internet to see when Blink would tour again, but sadly they never came to town, let alone to the East Coast.

However, years ago back on May 30, 2004, my buddy Mike and I went to Darien Lake Theme Park. Darien Lake was running a promotion that if you brought a specially marked pop can, you would receive a discounted park admission after 5pm. That afternoon when Mike and I went to Darien Lake, there was a concert at Darien Lake's Performing Arts Center, with Blink 182 headlining.

Mike and I rode rides that afternoon until the park closed. As Mike and I left the park and walked through the parking lot to the car, we could hear Blink 182 playing to the thousands of their fans. Though officially Mike and I did not see Blink 182 in concert, we heard them play.

Pretty Fly for a White Guy

Now, I love the Offspring. Who doesn't love the Offspring? They are Southern California's best Punk band, period. There may be some of you out there who disagree with me and might think that Green Day is Sunny CA's best punk band, but let me remind you that the Offspring still refuses to wear eye liner. So, getting back to my story…

I can remember back in the mid-90s when my older sister Sarah got her hands on *Smash*, the Offspring's breakthrough album. I remember Sarah constantly blasting *"Come Out and Play."* The opening lines were "You gotta keep em separated!" and that song just pissed mom off to no extent. I always thought that it was so awesome when the song was played over the speakers at the Buffalo Sabres games when Rob "Rayzor" Ray, Brad "May Day" May, or Matt "the Brat" Barnaby would get into a scuffle or fight with some dude on the opposing team.

I remember *Smash* being awesome as a kid, and learning new swear words from it. Many in my family can attribute my current cussing finesse roots to *Bad Habit*. If you don't know what I'm referring to, then listen to the song…it's an oldie, but a goodie.

Then in 97, the Offspring came out with *Ixnay on the Hombre*, which was another one of mom's "favorite" CDs. Mom thought the Offspring was evil because *Ixnay* had cartoon skulls on the CD cover!

Ixnay was cool, and I remember hearing it quite vividly though the bedroom walls because Sarah always had that shit cranked!

1998 brought my favorite Offspring album of all time, *Americana*. How anyone can not like *Americana* is beyond me! Sarah played the shit out of *Americana* so many times that she needed to replace the CD. And just like the previous two Offspring CDs, Sarah cranked the shit out of *Americana*. She blasted and listened to *Americana* so much that she blasted out the speakers to her Sony 5 disc CD player…mom and dad had a few days of peace and quiet until Sarah got another CD player, and then it was back to hearing such modern day classics such as *Pretty Fly (For a White Guy), The Kids Aren't Alright,* and *Why Don't You get a Job?*

I do have to say when I finally got my '87 Chevy El Camino Conquista, I blasted the crap out of *Pretty Fly (For a White Guy)* because I thought that I was pretty fly, cruising around in my El Camino.

So fast forward to Saturday July 28, 2012, Rochester, NY.

The Offspring were coming back to town! The Offspring were on tour plugging their newest album, *Days Go By*.

Now this upcoming Offspring show wasn't my first Offspring rodeo.

I saw them back in 2003 at the Dome Theater in Niagara Falls USA when the Offspring was touring in support of *Splinter*.

Then in 2005 I saw them again in the Vans Warped Tour at Darien Lake.

In 2009, they came to CMAC in Canandaigua, NY; touring in support of *Rise and Fall, Rage and Grace*.

Rochester's New Rock First, the Zone at 94.1 was putting on the concert in partnership with Scion's Bonzai concert series. The venue was the Highland Bowl, which was the same area where Rochester has its annual Lilac Festival.

The Offspring was the headliner with musical guests, Walk the Moon, Oberhofer, Eve 6, the Gaslight Anthem, and Our Lady Peace.

Shannon and I were meeting up with my friend Jeff and his girlfriend Elissa.

The concert started at noon, but Shannon and I were running a little late.

I gave Jeff a call to see where he was. Jeff answered his phone and told me he was in line for the show and the line was about a half mile long! I said, "Holy shit!" Jeff said, "Yea, no shit!" I told Jeff that Shannon and I were going to be on the road shortly.

Jeff called me a few minutes later after he got into the venue. I asked Jeff how difficult it was to sneak contraband into the show. Jeff said that it was extremely difficult because security was checking everybody and everything. He reported that the only thing we could bring in were blankets and lawn chairs. The light bulb in my head went off. I asked Jeff if they had brought lawn chair, and he had not. Shannon and I had a few captains' chairs that pack up nicely in their own bags. We decided to attempt to sneak a few beer cans into the show by concealing then in the bags.

It was probably around 1:00pm or so when Shannon and I parked the 2003 Dodge "Shaggin' Wagon" Caravan at the venue parking lot. There, Shannon drank her Dark and Stormy beverage and I chocked down a warm Labatt Blue. After our drinks had evaporated, we wandered into the show.

Shannon and I made it down to will call and got our tickets. By that time, there was no huge line to get into the show. Shannon and I walked up to security, they saw that we had lawn chairs, and let us in without being groped, frisked, or molested.

Shannon and I spotted Jeff and Elissa immediately. We chit chatted for a little bit before we wandered up to the merchandise tent. At the merch tent, there was the entire discography of the Offspring for sale, including a couple imported singles. I was hoping that they were going to have a live album of some sort.

There were a few bands out there like moe. and Pearl Jam, where minutes after the show ended, one could purchase a jump drive or CD of the set. Now, I thought that was a great idea! Almost every show I had been to, the band did not do that. I thought it was a little stupid on the band's part, because that was extra revenue that they were missing out on. Needless to say, the Offspring were not offering that day's show for purchase.

Since we got there a little late, Shannon and I thankfully missed one of the many shitty openers.

Jeff, Elissa, Shannon, and I decided to utilize the lawn chairs that we had brought. We made camp in the lawn, about 60 yards or so away from the stage. At the time, the weather conditions were a little muggy, but overcast. There was a slight breeze that was coming through that made it bearable. The other thing that made it bearable was the round of Labatt Blue that I picked up for everyone.

Eventually some radio DJs from the Rover's Morning Glories morning talk show took the stage and introduced Eve 6. Eve 6 was promoting their latest album, *Speak in Code*. I was not the biggest Eve 6 fan. I remember hearing them on the radio, but never got into them. I did not have their new album, let alone any of their albums, but I think it would be a safe assumption to say that they played a couple cuts off their new record. However, I did recognize two songs that they played. The one song was *Think Twice* and their closer was *Inside Out*.

Once Eve 6 left the stage, the four of us were getting hungry. Papa Johns had a pizza booth there, so Shannon and I picked up a pizza pie for everyone to munch on. I think Papa John should change his slogan from "Better Ingredients. Better Pizza." To "Shitty Ingredients. Shittier Pizza." Though I thought of myself as a pizza connoisseur, Papa John's did not rank high in my book.

Gaslight Anthem was next on the bill. Gaslight was plugging their 4th album, *Handwritten,* which had just come out that week. I was not big into Gaslight. The Zone @ 94.1 played the shit out them and a whole bunch of other shitty no namers, so I couldn't tell you what they played, but it was whiney.

By this point in time, the weather had changed slightly. The clouds have moved on and the sun was beating down on us. The four of us packed up our chairs and wandered over into the shade.

We were parched again, so Jeff and Elissa picked up the next round of brews. Tell you what, the Highland Bowl was an alright venue; it was small and intimate. There were three beer tents and just one set of bathrooms. There were 2 port-a-potties and a bathroom truck, so taking a leak sucked and took forever. Thankfully Our Lady Peace sucked, so I had no problem taking a piss during their set.

I was not the biggest fan of the Canadian band. I couldn't stand their whiny, nasally drone. Growing up in Buffalo, right on the Canadian border, OLP was overplayed on the US and Canadian air waves. Not to mention, Shannon and I suffered through watching them at Edgefest up in Toronto at the Molson Canadian Amphitheater back on July 1, 2006.

Regardless, Shannon and I survived another hour long set of Our Lady Peace. Like every other band at Bonzai, OLP was plugging their latest album, *Curve.* I wasn't sure if they played some material off of it, but honestly, I could care less what they played. Shannon and I were only there for the good company, people watching, and the Offspring!

People watching at the show was just alright. Even though we were watching a Canadian band, we did not see any mullets; go figure! People watching was *just* alright, nothing to write home about.

OLP played a few songs that we knew, such as *Superman's Dead, Clumsy,* and *Starseed.* Our Lady Peace finished off their set with *Some Where Out There.*

While the four of us were waiting in the shade for the Offspring, I could hear a distinct buzzing noise. I turned around and saw a Hep C/HIV tent! The Hep C/HIV tent was a full sized snow mobile trailer for tattooing. Now if I was going to get a tattoo, it sure as hell wasn't going to be in the Hepatitis tent or HIV trailer at a rock concert. Jeff and I then joked about getting matching "13" tattoos, but knowing our luck, we would probably get a "31".

It was finally 7:15pm and my beloved Offspring took to the stage.

The Offspring kicked off their set list with *The Future is Now*, which was a new song off their 9th and latest album, *Days Go By.* I was not 100% sure, but I thought their next song was *Secrets From the Underground*, which is also off the new album.

For the Offspring's third song, lead guitarist, Noodles, stepped up to the microphone and said, "You gotta keep 'em separated!" the opening lines to *Come Out and Play.* At this point in time, the Highland Bowl went crazy and there was a huge rush of crowd surfers. One of the many beach balls going around wound up on stage, and the band booted it back out to the ballistic crowd.

I asked Jeff what he wanted the Offspring to play. Jeff was an Offspring purest and loved their early hard punk work, so Jeff naturally wanted to hear stuff off their first two albums; *The Offspring* and *Ignition.* Unfortunately for Jeff, the Offspring did not play anything off their first two albums.

I asked Elissa what she wanted to hear, and she was just happy to see the Offspring.

I asked Shannon what she wanted to hear. Shannon shouted out, "Oh don't pick up the soap!" Shannon was referring to *When You're in Prison*, which can be found on track 12 off of *Splinter.* To Shannon's dismay, the Offspring did not play that song either.

Like Elissa, I was just happy and thrilled to see the Offspring again.

Jeff asked me if there was any song in particular that I wanted to hear. I told Jeff, "Yea, all of them. They are going to play all their staples, so I wouldn't mind hearing some rare stuff. I'm fine with anything off of Americana. I wouldn't mind hearing their new song *Cruising California (Bumpin' in My Trunk)*" Sadly, the Offspring did not play that song either.

Even though the Offspring did not play the songs we wanted, they did not disappoint! They played everything else we wanted to hear. The first part of their set consisted of a lot of songs off of *Americana* including *Have You Ever, Staring at the Sun, The Kids Aren't Alright, Walla Walla, Americana, Why Don't You Get a Job?* and *Pretty Fly (For a White Guy)*.

Shannon liked *Pretty Fly* because her hero Weird Al did a parody of that song, *Pretty Fly for a Rabbi*.

During the Offspring's set, I leaned over to Jeff and asked, "Hey, why is Dexter (lead singer) wearing sun glasses? It's not like he's staring into the sun? Its 7:45 and the sun has already set!" Jeff just chuckled.

With the exception of their first two albums, the Offspring played at least one song off of every album. We got to listen to *You're Gonna Go Far, Kid* and *Kristy, Are You Doing Okay?* from *Rise and Fall, Rage and Grace*.

Dexter Holland came up to the mic and said something along the lines of, "Hey Rochester! How are you doing? We love you guys and your support! We love you guys and I think we should come back here and play every week!" The Highland Bowl just ate it up and everyone cheered, including the four of us. I turned to Shannon and said, "Well they better come back, because I hate waiting every three years to see them!"

The Offspring continued to play some more, pump you up, ass kicking songs such as *Bad Habit, Want You Bad,* and *Hit That*.

Dexter told the crowd, "We're gonna play a new song and it's the title track off our new record" and the band broke into *Days Go By*.

The Offspring played a few more songs including *Gotta Get Away*. After that, the Offspring left the stage. Some of the concert goers started to leave. I looked down at my phone and it was only a little after 8pm. I looked around too and noticed that two out of the three beer tents were still open. I just chuckled to myself and said, "Novices, show's not over."

Sure as shit, the Offspring came back on stage for an encore. I figured the encore was going to last at least another hour considering that the beer tents were open. Well, I was wrong. The Offspring closed their set with *All I Want* and *Self Esteem.*

By the time the show ended, it wasn't even 8:30pm and the sun was still out! The Offspring still had another hour left of material to play, like *Gone Away*! And not to mention, the beer tents were still open!

The beer tents that were still opened were trying to get rid of the beer they had already poured. The beer was BoGo. Now "Old Adam" would have been all over that shit and bought three rounds worth, but "Older, '*Wiser*' Adam" figured that it would not be a good idea.

Jeff, Elissa, Shannon, and I waited for the crowd of 2,000 to die down a bit before we made our way out.

I was still pumped on just seeing the Offspring, that I asked Jeff, "Hey do you want to go out to Syracuse tomorrow and see the Offspring and Korn at K-Rock-a-thon?"

Jeff replied with, "Being from Syracuse, you don't want to go to K-Rock-a-thon, because there's a good possibility of getting shanked."

90s Revival

Summerland 2012 (suhm-er-land-twen-tee-twelv) *noun* 1. 1990s rock revival tour created by Mark McGrath (founder of Sugar Ray) and Art Alexakis (founder of Everclear). 2. Lineup includes Marcy Playground, Lit, Gin Blossoms, Sugar Ray, and Everclear. 3. Retro is in.

Summerland Tour 2012 was originally scheduled for Sahlen's Stadium in Rochester, New York on Thursday July 26, 2012. The show was rescheduled for that following Monday, July 30th. The reason why the show was rescheduled was due to the fact that there might have been a huge rain storm pending. You see, the Summer of 2012 had been one of the driest summers on record. There had been no rain fall in the entire month of July in Western New York. Nationally, it was the most severe drought in 25 years.

The night before the concert, Western New York experienced a torrential down pour, which was good. It rained so much on Wednesday that meteorologists were predicting the rain to carry over all day into Thursday. So that's the reason why the show got bumped to the following Monday.

98.9 The Buzz, one of Rochester's many crappy radio stations, was promoting the concert. On the radio, the station advertised that the show was starting promptly at 5pm.

Getting to Sahlen's Stadium by 5pm was no problem for Shannon and me. Shannon already had the day off from work and I was home from Jury Duty by 3:30pm.

Shannon and I left the house by 4pm to make it to the show on time. We left fairly early because we had a few factors that we needed to play with.

First of all, Shannon and I needed to stop off at Delta Sonic to pick up some cash from the ATM and to pick up some beverages of the alcoholic kind. I ended up grabbing a couple Sparks because they were 8%, and they would help to get us a buzz quicker than beer.

Second, we had to navigate rush hour traffic.

Third, we needed to find parking for the venue, Sahlen's Stadium.

If we could pause for a second, I'd like to take some time to describe to you what Sahlen's Stadium is. Sahlen's Stadium (formerly known as PAETEK Park, and then Marina Auto Stadium) is a soccer field located in one of the ghettos of Rochester; a perfect place to have a 1990s white folk rock revival concert.

Shannon and I ended up parking the 2003 Dodge "Shaggin' Wagon" Caravan at a parking lot shared by Kodak and Frontier Field (home of the Rochester Red Wings AAA baseball team). Yes, Kodak was still around in 2012, but just barely.

Any who, after we parked, it was 4:45pm. Shannon and I quickly chugged our Sparks, while trying to hide them from the Kodak Security rent-a-cop who was parked nearby.

Once we polished off our brews, we walked the three blocks down Oak Street to Sahlen's Stadium.

Shannon and I passed through the turn styles at 5pm on the dot. As we looked around the stadium, we noted that it was completely dead! There may have been 100 people there.

Shannon had to pee, so I followed suit.

Next I found the beer tent and bought me one Molson Canadian beer, or as they say in French, *Molson Canadian Biere.*

Then we made our way to the bleachers that were in the shade.

The stage was set up behind the goal, off of the field. We were permitted to go onto the field, but most of it was closed off. We could only walk around the goal keepers box area.

Shannon and I waited for the show to start. The first band was supposed to take the stage at 5pm, but they never did.

It was soon 5:30pm and then 5:45pm. I was getting a little rambunctious by this point. Shannon and I had wasted almost an hour in the stadium and nothing was going on. I told Shannon, "They are charging $7 for beer here…I could run back to the car, pound some beer back at the van, and buy another ticket at the box office for $20, and still make out like a bandit and have a cheaper beer bill at the end of the night…"

Shannon was not opposed with me running back to the van to execute *Operation Cheaper Beer*, but as 6pm struck, Mark McGrath and Art Alexakis took the stage to greet all 125 of us fans.

The boys thanked us all for coming out in support of the show and they were glad to see us, even though the show was postponed. Mark went on to say how he and Art got the idea a few years back to have a summer concert series of a whole bunch of washed up 90s bands. I personally think that Mark was getting bored of doing reality TV for VH1 and wanted to go back on tour.

Marcy Playground took the stage shortly after 6pm. They played a few songs, which nobody knew, mainly because they were a one hit wonder. Marcy Playground finished their set of 7 songs by 6:30pm. They ended their set with their only radio hit, *Sex and Candy*. All 138 of us gave an enthusiastic clap and cheer when they finished.

The set change didn't take too long, considering that Lit had their instruments already on stage, right behind Marcy's shit.

During the set change, Shannon and I visited the beer cart again. There were slim pickings for beverage…Molson, Coors Light, or Mike's Hard. Shannon and I opted for the Mike's Hard because they were 8% alcohol vs. the beer, which was about 3 or 4%...this was just another fine example of Shannon and I being wise consumers and getting more bang for our buck.

The time was a few ticks before 7pm when our hosts Mark and Art took to the stage to introduce the next band, Lit.

I remember Lit from my youth, but I never really got into them. I knew they were more than a one hit wonder, but I didn't remember how many radio hits they had. As the band took the stage, the guitarist and bassist were rocking fedora hats. The lead singer, A. Jay Popoff, followed them out and was dressed like a weirdo. He was wearing tight black jeans that were rolled up. He also had a couple of chains on his jeans and he was wearing black boots…he was dressed like he was a part of the 1970 underground Punk movement, looking something like the Sex Pistols…In other words, his clothing style did not match the rest of the band and their fedoras.

Anyway, back to the music.

Lit played one of their radio hits that I recognized, *Miserable*. Lit played some other stuff as well, but as I said earlier, I never got into them, so I can't tell you what else they played off hand. I can tell you that they were promoting their latest album, *The View From the Bottom*, and they played a cut from it.

I do have to say that watching A. Jay perform was quite entertaining. He reminded me of Scott Weiland from Stone Temple Pilots in that A. Jay pranced around the stage and stripped down, just like Scotty boy did.

Lit ended their set with their most famous song, *My Own Worst Enemy*. By this point, all 253 fans cheered and sang along with the band.

During the set change, Shannon and I visited the beer cart again to replenish our Mike's Hard.

Mark and Art came back out on stage to introduce the next band, Gin Blossoms. Gin Blossoms started off their set with one of their hits, *Follow You Down*.

Just like Lit, I knew of the Gin Blossoms, but never got too big into them, however I can recognize their stuff on the radio. Surprisingly Shannon knew more Gin Blossoms songs than I did.

Gin Blossoms ended up playing *Found Out About You* and a bunch of other songs I did not know, but Shannon knew them. Gin Blossoms ended their set with their biggest and break through song *Hey Jealousy*.

During the next set change, Shannon and I, yet again, visited the cart. By this time, Shannon and I had sampled all three flavors of the Mike's Hard product line; Lemonade, Cranberry Lemonade, and Black Cherry Lemonade. All three were delicious, tasty, and getting the job done!

In the meantime, we spotted one of our friends, Wendy. Wendy was inside the VIP area. Shannon and I called her over to chitchat. Wendy whispered into our ears, "Here's an extra ticket to get into the VIP section. See if it works." Wendy slipped me a ticket through the fence and I walked around to the entrance of the VIP section. I walked in without a problem. I quickly met up with Shannon and handed off the ticket. Moments later, the 3 of us were hanging out in the VIP section. The VIP section allowed those with VIP tickets to be front and center of the stage! Shannon was thrilled.

Next on the bill was Shannon's favorite, Sugar Ray!

I'm gonna pause for a quick TV timeout…quick little tid bit of knowledge; Shannon's 1st concert was Sugar Ray…And now back to our regularly scheduled programming!

Mark McGrath kicked off Sugar Ray's set with *Every Morning* and all the grown up teeny boppers went crazy, including Shannon.

I do have to say that in my youth, I got into Sugar Ray for a little bit. I remember "borrowing" Sugar Ray's *Floored* album (CD) from my older sister Sarah. I enjoyed *Fly* and *Stand and Deliver*.

Mark McGrath was pumping up the crowd in white skin tight jeans, white tee shirt, black vest, and his spiked frosted tips; it was like he never left the 90s.

I did notice that Sugar Ray was lacking one person from their original line up, the token black guy, better known as DJ Homicide. I felt a little gypped that DJ Homicide wasn't there!

Anyway, back to the concert. Mark McGrath went through the usual ropes and thanked everyone for being there and played a few more songs that I did not recognize, but Shannon knew almost all of them.

Midway through their set, Mark McGrath called up 2 dudes from the crowd to have a sing off competition. The band played improv to House of Pain's *Jump Around* while the one dude had to beat box it. The dude did surprisingly well and knew all the words. The other dude had to sing a Lady Gaga or Kelly Clarkson song, which the dude shockingly knew the words to. Both guys won and got free concert shirts. I thought that was pretty cool. It made the band seem that much more personable and in touch with reality.

During Sugar Ray's set, Mark threw out a guitar pick into the crowd. Shannon extended her arm out to grab the pick, but it bounced off her palm, and onto the ground. Shannon ended up wrestling some wildebeest chick for the guitar pick! That made Shannon's night.

Sugar Ray ended their set *Fly* and all the 20 and 30 something year old teeny boppers went wild.

Finally it was time for Everclear!

Tell you what, Art Alexakis looked old! And his receding hair line and wrinkles didn't help either. Everclear took the stage during the opening melody to *So Much for the Afterglow*.

Everclear kicked off their set with *Father of Mine*. I leaned over to Shannon and said, "How fitting, considering we're in the ghetto."

Everclear's next song was *Everything to Everyone*. Now I am definitely one to say, "If it's too loud, then you're too old" but Everclear had the music cranked so loud, that the music was coming out distorted.

Art was the only original member of Everclear that night. I'm sure that if Art went under his real name, Art Alexakis, everyone would have been, "Art who?" But since Art still tours under Everclear, he had a better turn out.

Next on Everclear's set list was *AM Radio, Heroin Girl, Volvo Driving Soccer Mom,* and *I Will Buy You A New Life.*

Everclear was also touring in support of their latest album *Invisible Stars* and played *Be Careful What You Ask for.*

Everclear played *Wonderful* before going into a mini Led Zeppelin melody. Art ripped off a few chords of a Zeppy song and said something along the lines of, "Ah, we're not a cover. We're not gonna play that shit."

Art looked at the crowd and asked us what we wanted to hear. Naturally I yelled, "Freebird!" which was followed up by many others yelling the same.

Art then looked back behind to the drummer and asked him what he wanted to play. The drummer broke into the opening drum line to Led Zeppelin's *Rock and Roll.* Art started playing the few opening notes to the song. Everclear played *Rock and Roll* for about 15 seconds before Art stopped and said, "Like I said earlier, we're not a cover band."

Then Art played the opening riff to *Santa Monica* and everyone cheered and bounced around. Suddenly band members from Marcy Playground, Lit, and Gin Blossoms came out to help Art sing *Santa Monica.* Unfortunately Mark McGrath did not come out. It was pretty cool seeing 15 or so musicians up on stage singing. *Santa Monica* turned out to be Everclear's closer.

Once the show was over, Shannon and I parted ways with Wendy.

Both Shannon and I were starving, so we decided to have dinner at one of our favorite hot spots, Empire Hots for a cheeseburger Trash Plate!

Twins of Evil

T'was Tuesday October 16, 2012, around 5pm or so.

I had just arrived home from a long 8 hour shift of work.

I decided to grab a can of beer to unwind and relax on the can. Man, there's nothing more relaxing than plopping your ham on the can and opening a cold one. In case you were wondering what brew I was drinking. Well, it goes by many names, such as a Genny Screamer, a Scream Ale, a Genny Green Monster, call it what you will, but it's real name is Genesee Cream Ale….and it has those nicknames for a reason. It goes in nice and creamy and frothy, and it comes out nice and creamy and frothy!

Now I have this ritual that I've been doing as far back as I can remember, I poop and then I shower. I'm not a fan of skid marks in my undies and I like to be clean down in my nether region. You never know when something is going to come up, and I would just like to be clean and prepared down there if anything happens…if you know what I mean.

I timed my drinking on the can such that when I finished my beer, it was time to wipe, and hop into the shower.

Once I had satisfactorily cleaned myself, I hopped out of the shower and got prepared for the Twins of Evil show at the Main Street Armory in downtown Rochester.

One Mr. Marilyn Manson and one Mr. Rob Zombie were co-headlining the Twins of Evil Tour. They had a special guest, J Devil (Jonathan Davis from Korn) mixing on the turn tables as the opener. It was built up to be an awesome show just weeks before Halloween!

Shannon and I have seen Rob Zombie a few times before. The first time we saw him, he co-headlined with Godsmack at Darien Lake back in 2006. We saw Zombie a few years later with Alice Cooper on the *Gruesome Twosome Tour* at Artpark in Lewiston, NY in 2010. Both shows were beyond awesome and phenomenal and we both vowed to see Rob anytime he came close to town.

Now I have never seen Marilyn Manson before. Back in high school, Manson was at his prime. Many people, like my mom, thought that Manson was the antichrist. Anyway, I heard from a couple close sources that Manson put on a great stage show, and that was why I was excited to see him.

And lastly, who doesn't like Jonathan Davis from Korn? Korn is kick ass and so is J Devil.

By the time I got dressed, the wife had arrived home from work. She did not have to poop or shower. All she did was changed out of her work clothes into some street clothes.

The doors to the Main Street Armory were to be opened at 6pm and J Devil was supposed to go on around 7pm.

Shannon and I hopped into the 2003 Dodge Caravan at 6:15pm.

It was 6:45pm when Shannon and I drove past the Main Street Armory. Surprisingly, we saw that the doors to the Armory were still closed shut. There was a line of people from the main doors, down the stairs, and down Main Street. Shannon and I looked at each other and both agreed that that was weird.

After we passed the Armory, we drove around to try to find parking. There were a couple tiny parking lots by the Armory and the Rochester Auditorium Theater, but all the lots were filled.

We drove around some back roads behind the Armory, but if we parked there, it looked like we would have been sodomized and murdered. We pressed on for better parking.

It took us a few minutes, but we were able to find parking underneath a working light pole on Alexander Street and Main Street.

Shannon and I glanced down at the clock in the shaggin' wagon and noticed that it was only 7pm. Shannon was not too thrilled that there was an opener. We both agreed that if we wasted a few minutes in the van pounding beers, then that should help let the line in front of the Armory die down.

Tailgating is just like eating a Lays potato chip, in that you just can't have one. Well, one turned into two, which turned into three, and then I had to pee. I found a tree in a vacant lot next to the van.

After I relieved myself, we looked at the clock and noticed that it was only 7:10. Shannon and I decided that it was best if we split one last beer, just to make sure that the line had died down.

Once we polished off that last beer, I asked Shannon if she wanted me to bring in the plastic baby bottle of Fighting Cock Whiskey. She looked at it and contemplated out loud, "Um…no. I'm leaning towards no because we just pounded a few of those brews and I'm already feeling it. The Hot Pocket apparently isn't sopping anything up...I don't have much in my stomach, and I think that's going to make me sick..." So we opted to not take the whiskey.

Shannon and I made our way down Alexander Street to the intersection of Main Street. We walked down Main Street a bit before crossing the road. It was a brisk cool night, but nothing too cold.

As we approached the Main Street Armory, Shannon and I saw a huge line from the Armory door, come down Main Street, go into an adjacent lot, and the line of people snake tailed around itself!

Shannon and I looked at each other in disbelief and said, "You gotta be fucking kidding me!"

We had no other choice but to hop in the back of the line. Shannon and I paid well over $100 for these tickets and we were going to be damned if we left without seeing the show!

By the time we found the back of the line, it was probably 7:20pm.

As we painfully waited in line, the beers started to take their toll on me. Since I inherited my mom's bladder, it was only 5 minutes before I had to pee. Thankfully we were in a quasi-light parking lot.

Before I ventured off into the dark parking lot, I told Shannon that I had to see a man about a horse.

I soon found a late model Chevy pickup truck, red in color, to pee behind. As I whipped my moose cock out to pee, I could hear a couple female voices yelling at me. It was dark, so I had no idea where they were coming from. All I heard was, "Can you give us a little privacy?!"

I responded, "Sorry ladies. It's dark, I didn't see you..." What I really wanted to say was, "Sorry ladies, I didn't see you because my huge moose cock was in the way!" Instead, I readjusted and decided to aim the opposite way.

Then I heard another female voice saying, "Excuse me! I'm trying to pee here!"

I told her, "Uh...I don't know where your voice is coming from, but I'm sorry."

It was very dark and cold out. The ladies could not even see my giant moose cock so I apologized to whoever owned the red Chevy pickup, but I peed next to it and I may have gotten some back splash on the tire. If it was a Toyota, I would have pissed all over the fucking thing and not cared. I probably would have saved my dump if it was a Toyota.

After I was relieved, I found Shannon back in line…She was still in the same spot as I had left her minutes before. I say minutes before because there was a lot of fluid to expel.

By the time the line had made from the snake coil in the adjacent parking lot to Main Street, Shannon was regretting that I hadn't grabbed that baby bottle of whiskey. I told Shannon a few times that I would walk back to the shaggin' wagon to get it, but she was too nervous for my safety.

We had finally made it to the front of the Main Street Armory and it had felt like forever! Shannon and I had already waited in line for over 45 minutes!

Just then a security guard said, "Hey. We are letting people in the side entrance over here!"

Shannon and I looked at each other and contemplated it for a few seconds. We saw a huge flood of people rush over to the side entrance, so we decided to follow suit.

By the time we reached the side entrance, security was forcing us back to Main Street, telling us that they weren't letting people in.

Shannon and I were in agreement, "You gotta be (explitive) kidding me! You have a concert that doors open at 6pm…You have an opener at 7pm…the venue doesn't even open the doors until after 7pm! You have a huge angry mob of people outside the venue that want to come in! Horrible set up! Horrible planning!"

Shannon and I walked past the security guard that directed us toward the side entrance. Shannon said, "They aren't letting us in down there!"

The security guard said, "Well you have to get back in line."

Shannon said, "I'm gonna be damned if I have to get into the back of the line after waiting close to an hour already."

So Shannon and I resumed our spots that we originally had in line.

About 10 minutes later, that same douche bag security guard said that the side entrance was re-opened and accepting hard copy tickets. I looked at Shannon and said, "Fuck that! I'm just gonna wait here in line. We are almost there! I can see the steps!"

Probably 10 minutes later, Shannon and I were being frisked before we entered the Armory.

Once we entered the venue, Shannon asked the ticket taker, "What was the hold up?! Why did it take so long for everyone to get in?!"

The ticket taker said, "It was the manager. The manager screwed up and got the bands here late."

Honestly, I don't care whose fault it was! Just open the fucking door when you say you're going to!

You mean to tell me as the owner of a concert venue, you are not going to open doors on time and miss out on merchandise and beer sales? That sounds like poor economics to me!

And to top it off, we missed the opener and half of Marilyn Manson!

When we finally got into the venue, it was well past 8:30pm and Manson was performing *The Dope Show*.

As I mentioned earlier, I have my mom's and bladder. Shannon has the bladder of a camel. However, we both decided it was time to pee.

One we finished peeing, we rendezvoused in the beer line. At this point in time, Marilyn Manson was prancing around the stage to *Slo-Mo-Tion* and *Rock Is Dead*.

Once Shannon and I each got our two Labatt Blues, we meandered into the crowd. The Main Street Armory was mainly standing room only. There was a balcony that wrapped around ¾ of the perimeter, but those seats were already filled. Shannon and I found a spot where Shannon could see through all the tall people. I had texted our buddy Kirk that we finally made it into the venue and that we finally had beer again. Manson then played two songs that I really enjoy, though they were both covers, Depeche Mode's *Personal Jesus* and Eurythmics' *Sweet Dreams (Are Made of This)*. I have to say that Manson's covers are better than the originals.

In the meantime, tall people started to stand in front of Shannon. I don't know what it is about her, but it always happens; without fail at every concert we go to. I noticed that the back of the venue was completely open from people. So we walked back there. We stood next to the merchandise table and we had a great view of the stage. Beside us was a bar that was not being used, so Shannon decided to sit on top of the bar for an even better view.

Then, the stage was lit up with blue lights and a singular spot light was on Manson. Manson was wearing all black and an Amish hat. From the spot light, you could see "snow" or confetti being drizzled upon Manson as he sang *Coma White*.

Manson played *Killing 33°*, and *Antichrist Superstar*. He finished his set with *The Beautiful People*...Rah!

Shannon and I enjoyed our Marilyn Manson experience, but we both thought he was going to be a little bit better. I think a few of my friends hyped him up.

As the roadies took the stage to break it down and set up for Rob Zombie, our buddy Kirk came over to hang out with us.

Shannon and I asked Kirk where his girlfriend Jess was. Kirk said that she was up closer to the front of the stage and that she didn't want to hang out. Oh well, no big loss.

In the meantime one of my Labatt Blues had evaporated. I noticed that Kirk was empty handed. I asked Kirk if he wanted to wait in the really long beer line for some moderately priced beer. Kirk said, "Of course!"

It took Kirk and me a while to grab a round of beer. We then met back up with Shannon. Shannon had struck up a conversation with this dude named Philip. Philip was also stuck in the huge cluster-f mess of a line outside. Philip, a black kid, said that he was a huge Marilyn Manson fan. He said back in the day, he used to have pirated copies of Manson's music on cassette tapes. His mom disapproved of Manson because she thought he was evil and the antichrist. Needless to say, his mom threw out his cassettes. Philip said that he would have the kids at school make him more tapes or burned CDs. Philip said that he went to a city school and all his friends, who were black, made fun of him for loving Marilyn Manson, and thought he was weird for listening to rock. They couldn't understand why he wasn't listening to DMX, Puffy Daddy, Jay-Z, 2Pac, or Notorious B.I.G. Philip said that he got into the venue just in time to see Manson perform his favorite song, *Antichrist Superstar*. I asked Philip if he had ever seen Rob Zombie before and he said that he had not. I told him that he was in for a treat!

Minutes later, the house lights went out, and everyone cheered. *Sinner Inc.* was being played overhead. The TV monitors flashed the letters R-O-B-Z-O-M-B-I-E on loop, while smoke and strobe lights went off. There was fire and brimstone, dogs and cats living together, mass hysteria! *Sinner Inc.* played right into *Demon Speeding* which was followed up by *Jesus Frankenstein.*

Rob took a second to talk to the crowd. He said that he was surprised at how small the stage was at the Amory and that they couldn't use all their props they brought. Rob reassured us that he was going to put on a good show for us.

Zombie then played *Meet the Creeper*, which was awesome! Zombie had one of his larger than life space aged creeper robots walking around the stage; it was spewing smoke out into the crowd.

Rob took another moment to talk to the audience. He told us that the next song was for the lovely ladies of Rochester, then the band broke into *Living Dead Girl.*

Next, Zombie and company played *More Human Than Human.* Zombie had another larger than life green robot alien dancing around the stage. The green robot alien looked the creature that was featured on the back cover of Rob Zombie's *Hillbily Deluxe* album. I wanted the job of being that green alien robot. I thought that it would be cool to tour with Rob Zombie and break it down on stage!

More Human Than Human was followed up by *Mars Needs Women.*

Then there was a mini drum solo and up on the TV monitors, Rob Zombie was playing clips from a new movie that he had just finished working on, *The Lords of Salem.* This was around the time when I had to piddle again because I had already broken the seal. As I entered the men's room, I walked to the nearest open stall. It was around this point in time when I had walked in on a drug deal gone bad. Security rushed into the men's room right behind me and some John flushed his smack down the shitter so he wouldn't get caught. Security hauled his ass away. There was a lot of security at that show. Every time I went to the bathroom to take a leak, there were always at least 2 or 3 security guards in or around the bathrooms.

Anyway, after I finished taking a leak, I washed my hands with soap, water, and friction. Then I returned to the bar where Shannon was sitting.

Never Gonna Stop (The Red, Red Kroovy) and *Sick Bubble-Gum* were next on the set list. *Sick Bubble-Gum* was awesome. At first, the TV monitors were showing clips of stupid anime. It was cool when they started to show clips of Charlie Brown from *The Great Pumpkin*. As the young kids say, it was off dah hook, when the Great Pumpkin took the stage and boogied around the band.

Once *Sick Bubble-Gum* ended, the Great Pumpkin left the stage. Zombie and company then played *Scum of the Earth* and one of my favorite songs, *Pussy Liquor*. During *Pussy Liquor*, scenes from Rob Zombie's movie, *House of 1000 Corpses* played on the TV monitors.

The Main Street Armory lit up when the first few thumping bass chords to *Thunder Kiss '65* were played.

Rob Zombie gave his fans that night a cover tune. He covered Alice Cooper's *School's Out* and it sounded great, almost too great. It was almost better than the original, but I can't make any comparisons because that would be comparing apples to oranges.

Sadly the show had to end. The closer was *Dragula* and the place went wild.

Once the show ended, Rob Zombie gave credits to his band members, stage crew, and his wife Sheri Moon Zombie. Everyone took a bow and exited the stage.

Rob Zombie was awesome, yet again. He put on another wonderful act and performance.

Once the show was over, Kirk's girlfriend Jess showed up. Shannon, Jess, Kirk, and I waited for the crowd to die down before we left the armory. Jess and Kirk parked 10 blocks away, so Shannon and I gave them a lift to their car.

After we dropped them off, Shannon and I had the munchies. Shannon and I opted for our post-concert retreat, Empire Hots for a Trash Plate! It only took a few seconds, but Shannon and I wolfed that cheeseburger plate down. Then it was bedtime! Though we were home and in bed before 11:30pm, it was extremely difficult to wake up at 6:45am for work the next day!

A Long, Crappy Evening

I thought I was a fan of Scott Weiland. Scott Weiland used to be the lead singer of Stone Temple Pilots and Velvet Revolver.

Shannon and I had seen STP and Velvet Revolver multiple times. I told myself, and probably Shannon, that whenever STP came to town, I would like to see them no matter what.

Every New Year, I was amazed that the heroin junkie Weiland had made it another year. As I had mentioned before, Scott was always in my Death Draft. It would be a safe bet to say that it would only be a matter of time before heroin gets the best of Weiland. With that being said, I wanted to see Weiland perform as often as I could.

Wednesday February 27, 2013. No, Scott wasn't pronounced dead or missing or anything morbid like that. On that Wednesday, Scott had been kicked out of Stone Temple Pilots. It didn't seem to faze Weiland, and a day later, he said it was a publicity stunt to increase ticket and record sales.

Regardless, Shannon and I had a hot date to see Scott Weiland and the Wildabouts at the Rapids Theater in Niagara Falls, USA on Monday March 4, 2013.

The show was being billed as *An Evening with Scott Weiland*. I had heard rumors that that show was a greatest hits tour and I also heard that he was going to perform STP's first two albums, *Core* and *Purple*, from cover to cover. Either way, the show sounded like it was going to be a great one!

According to the playbill, door opened at 6:30pm and the show started at 8pm.

From what I could find, there was no talk of an opener. I sphinctered that the show would start at 8pm with Scott taking the stage and playing for about two hours. The show would end around 10pm or so and Shannon and I would be home by before midnight. It sounded logical to Shannon and me.

Shannon and I left the Greater Rochester Area shortly after 6pm. We drove down The 90 to Buffalo. There we took The 290 to The 190 to The Robert Moses Parkway. We found parking right off Main Street and we soon found ourselves in line for the concert. Once I got done having my butthole finger blasted by security, I got to enter the Rapids Theatre.

After Shannon and I were inside, we bellied right up the bar. The bar was located front and center to the venue. Shannon had to piddle, so she gave me some cash to buy a round of drinks. I bought two Labatt Blue drafts.

Minutes later I got our drinks, I walked over to the women's room to wait for Shannon. As I waited, I took a few sips off Shannon's beer because I didn't want to accidently spill any beer. If I would have accidently spilled any beer and let it hit the floor that would have been alcohol abuse. So I took one for the team and drank her beer down to a normal safe level. While waiting, I noticed a merchandise table. I decided to look at the overpriced shit they were selling. I noticed that Scott Weiland was peddling some overpriced t shirts and CDs. I also notice some crap from a group named Miggs.

I thought to myself, "Ah crap! There's a shitty opener?! Well that fucking sucks! I wish I would have known! Then Shannon and I could have gotten dinner before the show, like Mighty Taco!"

Moments later, Shannon came out of the lavatory and saw me. She saw the merch table and asked me if I wanted any Scott Weiland paraphernalia. I told her no, and that I noticed that there was an opener.

Shannon said, "Damnit! Really?! Well that fucking sucks! We could have grabbed dinner before the show, like at Mighty Taco!"

"I know!" I exclaimed. "Looks like we can't do anything about it," I said.

I had to give Miggs credit. They did take the stage promptly at 8pm.

Shannon and I have never heard of Miggs before. They played a couple songs that sounded alright. A few songs into their set, Miggs performed a decent cover of Led Zeppelin's *Whole Lotta Love* with the drummer on vocals. The drummer was awesome and did not miss a beat. The guitarist was excellent and did not miss a chord. The crowd dug it.

What the crowd did not dig was most of the other songs Miggs played. I hate to say it, but you could hear people in the crowd talking louder than Miggs. It's not that Miggs sucked, but people were there for Scotty.

Miggs had a song that had the same sound and melody to *Coming to America* by Neil Diamond, but it was not a cover.

Miggs got the crowd back into it with a very good rock cover of the Righteous Brother's *Unchained Melody*. And in case you were wondering, yes, the entire audience belted out the high note when it came to screeching, "*I need your love!*"

Miggs played a few other songs no one recognized before ending on a Rolling Stone Cover, *Satisfaction*.

Miggs finally left the stage promptly at 8:45pm

The roadies were quickly on the stage by 8:46pm.

The roadies didn't have that much work to do considering that Scott Weiland and the Wildabouts gear was already on stage.

Miggs gear was off the stage well before 9pm.

Now I am going to pause for a moment for some station identification and a rant session...

Miggs left the stage at 8:45pm.

Scotty the douchebag didn't even take the stage 'til 10pm! It was a fucking work night for all of us but Scott didn't seem to care and it showed! I'll get to that in a second...

While Shannon and I wait the hour and 15 minutes for the heroin junkie to take the stage, we wondered why it took so long for Scott's scrawny ass to take the stage. We started to joke around with the fellas next to us that Scott had finally overdosed on the tour bus. We joked around how the band and roadies were trying to wake him up but realized that he was dead from heroin. We joked that the crew was trying to rig Scott's corpse together like *Weekend At Bernie's* because as the saying goes, *the show must go on!*

As the concert goers waited for Scott's lazy ass to take the stage, Shannon had to break the seal. Shannon came back double fisted with Labatt Blues.

As we anxiously waited for Scott and the Douchebags, I too had to break the seal.

After I peed, I came back with two Blues as well.

It didn't take a rocket scientist, but you could feel the tension build in the air that Scott was taking his sweet ass time. The dudes next to us said, "You know he's shooting up if he has his arms covered!"

It was a little before 10pm when a fat roadie came out on stage and dropped off the set lists to every band position. That really infuriated Shannon and myself. Those fuck wads had been jerking us off for the last hour and 15 minutes!

By the time Fart Knocker and the Douche Bags hit the stage, Shannon and I didn't really give a fuck! Apparently most of the Rapids Theatre did. It seemed like most of the people in attendance had not seen Scott or STP or Velvet Revolver before because they were all cheering in excitement.

Scott came out playing some song that I had not heard before. I found out that Scott played a cover of David Bowie's *The Jean Genie*. Shannon and I couldn't hear shit because the sound was cranked so high and it sucked.

At first sight of Scott, I figured he was well beyond wasted. He was in a grey three piece suit. The suit reflected silver when the stage lights hit it. He was also wearing sun glasses. I wasn't sure if he was wearing sunglasses because the stage lights were too bright or if he was so high that the bright lights distracted him.

Once Scott finished the opening song, he wandered over to the drum kit while proceeding to take off his coat and grabbed some water. Then he started to babble into the microphone about some incoherent bull shit. He was whining that the mic was cutting out and that he wanted a new mic. Scotty Toilet Paper revisited the drum kit for another slug of H2O. Then he did another, "Check check check" in to the mic. Scotty Toilet Paper wandered around a bit on stage before confronting the audience to tell us that he was going to play a song off of STP's 1st ablum...*Creep*.

The place lit up when Weiland sang *Creep*. I'm not going to lie; Scott's backup band was talented but they just don't have the authentic STP sound. No one can replace the DeLeo brothers and Eric Kretz.

Speaking of Weiland's backup band, the Wildabouts, they looked like an interesting bunch. The guitarist/keyboardist looked like the fat dude from the American version of *Top Gear* but with a longer pubic faced beard.

The bassist looked like Lou Diamond Philips, circa 1980s with his quasi mullet/long hair.

The other guitarist looked like a backup member in Weird Al's *Amish Paradise* band.

The drummer was hidden behind his drum kit and a shadow of darkness, so he was a mystery.

Scott babbled to the crowd that he was glad to be there or some shit like that. He told us that he liked the solo tours or something along those lines. He mentioned to us that he had a lot in store for us. He claimed that they were going to perform a lot of STP songs, along with some Velvet Revolver songs, and some others…needless to say, Scott never played a single Velvet Revolver song.

I don't think he was boozing it up before the show because he was able to stand, walk in a straight line, and talked coherently. Scotty just babbled between songs.

Weiland and his band played a few other STP classics like *Crackerman, Big Empty, Kitchenware & Candybars, Where the River Flows,* and *Still Remains.*

They also covered Jane's Addiction's *Mountain Song,* the Libertine's *Can't Stop Me Now,* and a Scott Weiland original, *Paralysis.*

Midway through the show, Scott said, "Here's a song named after a house hold product." The backup band tortured the opening notes to *Vaseline.*

Scott continued to ramble out gibberish in between songs. The band ended up playing *Interstate Love Song.* Once it ended, Scott told the audience something along the lines of, "Hey' we're gonna take a smoke break. We'll be right back." as he stumbled and sauntered his way off the stage.

By that point in time, Shannon and I were watching the show at the bar. Shannon turned around and looked at me. She said, "You have got to be (expletive that rhymes with 'ducking') kidding me! I can't believe people are putting up with this shit! He fucking sucks! He's wasted and sounds like shit and everyone is eating it up! No wonder STP kicked his stupid bo-tard ass out of the band! He sucks!"

I said, "Yea, I know, but I dunno what to tell you."

A few minutes passed by and surprisingly the band returned!

Suck Weiland and the Wildabouts returned to perform a Doors Cover, *Roadhouse Blues.* The set ended with *Sex Type Thing.* After that, the show was over.

Shannon and I were both extremely disappointed! It sounded like a horrible cruise ship cocktail lounge band where the band was slightly off key. Shannon and I were extremely dissatisfied and frustrated, especially after seeing Weiland perform twice in STP and Velvet Revolver.

By the time the show ended, it was 11:30pm! Shannon and I hopped back into our 2003 Dodge Caravan, with 210, 000 miles on it! By the time we made our way out of the Falls and onto the Robert Moses Parkway, it was close to midnight. By the time we hit Grand Island, Shannon and I were teetering on mid-night munchies. We really wanted to go to Mighty Taco on Grand Island, but I thought they would have been closed by the time we got there. Instead, Shannon and I opted for Plan B, Tim Hortons. Timmy Hos was always open, 24 hours!

Shannon and I stopped at the Timmy Hos on the Island. When we got to Time Hortons, Shannon got a hot chocolate and I got myself a coffee. I needed the coffee to keep me awake for the hour and a half ride back to the ROC.

It was almost 1:30am when we got back home, thanks to that freaking douchebag Scott Weiland and his lazy ass.

To my surprise, waking up at 6:45am on Tuesday wasn't that difficult. I grabbed another coffee at work, and I was fine until lunch. After lunch, I was ready for a nap or bed.

I will admit it, I was becoming an old fart. I worked my 8 hour day, punched out at 4:30ish, went home, and went to bed. I slept from 7pm to 7am.

Dookie

T'was April 1, 2013, April Fool's Day.

T'was April 1, 2013 and it was also Dyngus Day! If you aren't Polish, or don't live in a Polish community like Buffalo, then you have no idea what I am talking about. Well, Dyngus Day is a Polish holiday. It is always celebrated the day after Easter. It is to celebrate Easter and just another excuse for Polish people (and want-to-be Poles) to get drunk. Normally, girls chase around the boys they like and whip them with pussy willows. Boys chase girls around they like and squirt them with water. You can take that as a sexual connotation if you want to.

So anyways, it was April 1, 2013 and I was taking Shannon to a Green Day concert at the War Memorial in downtown Rochester, NY. The show was originally scheduled for a January date but it was postponed until April.

Before the show Shannon and I had a few beers to "pregame."

This wasn't our first time seeing Green Day. Back in 2005 we saw them at HSBC Arena in Buffalo while they were on their American Idiot tour. I recall the show was good, but only when they were playing their old stuff. We had floor tickets and we got pretty close to the stage. At the end of the show, the band was throwing guitar picks and drum sticks into the crowd. Shannon ended up getting hit in the head by a drum stick thrown by Tre Cool. Sadly Shannon unable to get the drum stick. While she was agonizing in pain, some kid ran up, picked the drum stick up off the ground, and took off.

Once inside the War Memorial, we grabbed a round of Molson and then found our seats. We bought the cheap seats as we did not want to fork over the extra money for the general admission in front of the stage. Additionally, Shannon is short and every time we got general admission tickets, Shannon could never see because the tallest person always stood in front of her.

Some scrub band was the opener. I couldn't even tell you who it was because they weren't that important.

Green Day was touring in support of their latest venture, a three album release. ¡Uno! was released in September 2012, followed by an October 2012 release of ¡Dos!, with third album

¡Tré! dropping that December 2012. Needless to say, up until that show, I had not heard a cut off the new albums. Honestly, Green Day should have stopped making music after their 2001 greatest hits release, *International Superhits!*

Moments before Green Day took the stage, a guy in a demonic and demented looking bunny rabbit outfit came out on stage and tried to hype up the crowd. Green Day soon made their grand entrance with the Ramones' *Blitzkrieg Bop* coming through on the speakers.

Lead singer and guitarist Billy Joe Armstrong said, "Hey Rochester! How are you doing?!" All the teeny boppers in the general admission section in front of the stage screamed like little school girls. Oh yeah, did I forgot to mention that Shannon and I were amazed by the amount of middle and high school kids there? Actually, Shannon and I felt like old farts, almost as if we were chaperones. There were quite a few people older than us at the show, but all us oldies were outnumbered by the teeny boppers—I was flabbergasted.

Even before Green Day played one song, Billy Joe asked the crowd at least three times, "Hey Rochester! How are you doing?!" Shannon and I decided to turn it into a drinking game!

I did not recognize Green Day's first song because it was written after Y2K; the Millennium. After the song, Billy Joe asked us again, "How you doing Rochester?!" Naturally Shannon and I took a sip from our beer.

Green Day played another song to the teeny boppers' liking. After that song, Billy Joe spiced things up a bit by saying, "Well, Buffalo is right down the road! Anybody from Buffalo here?! How are you doing Buffalo?!" I cheered because I'm from Buffalo. Billy Joe then asked how all the Rochesteriens we doing. Then he had a cheer –off to see if there were more Buffalo fans or Rochester fans; it was amusing.

After Green Day's third song, I said to Shannon, "I bet you a beer that he asks if there are any Syracuse people here!" Well I lost that bet to Shannon, though Billy Joe asked us again how the Buffalo and Rochester people were doing!

The first part of Green Day's set was all new crap. It's like the old saying goes, *new music sucks!* That was why I wanted Green Day to play their early shit.

While Green Day was playing their new crap, I noticed that the original three man group of Billy Joe, Mike Dirnt, and Tre Cool had a couple extra musicians on stage. Even though Billy Joe was briskly walking across the stage singing, his guitar was slung behind his back. It appeared that Green Day hired two back up guitarists to play the new crap.

During their set of new songs, Billy Joe picked a kid out of the audience to play his guitar for a song, which was pretty cool. I'm not sure what the song was, but I think it was *Letterbomb*.

Then Green Day played a couple tracks off their "Hand Grenade" album. While singing *Holiday*, Billy Joe switched the song's lyrics around. During *Holiday*, Billy Joe talks into a megaphone, "*The representative from California now has the floor...*" For us, Billy spoke into the megaphone, "*The representative from Buffalo-Rochester now has the floor!*" Shannon and I looked at each other, gave the nod, and we both kicked back a sip of some more beer!

I was not a huge fan of the "Hand Grenade" album; the only song worthwhile off of it was *Boulevard of Broken Dreams*, which thankfully they played.

After 30 minutes of white noise that sounded like Green Day music, Billy Joe finally asked where the real and original Green Day fans were. All us old farts put down our Metamucil and warm milk to cheer!

Green Day kicked off their old school set with *Burnout*.

Next Green Day played *Geek Stink Breath*. I remember when that music video was on MTV, back when MTV was cool and played music videos along with Beavis and Butt-Head. The music video isn't for the squeamish because it's about some dude who gets a molar tooth removed.

Geek Stink Breath was followed up by *Hitchin' a Ride* and *2000 Light Years Away*.

Then Green Day threw a wrench into the works and screwed up my middle school memory lane by playing some crap ass new song before playing *Brain Stew*. I love *Brain Stew*, it's probably one of Green Days best songs. I can remember being bored during study hall or class at St. Joe's Collegiate Institute when all of a sudden I would break out loud singing the guitar riffs of the song, "D*un nuh!*

Dun nuh! Dun nuh! Dun nuh dun nuh..." moments later, half of the class was humming or singing along!

On the album *Nimrod*, as the song *Brain Stew* ends, it meshes right into *Jaded*. However, during Green Day's performance of *Brain Stew*, they took some liberties and did not mesh into *Jaded*, but rather went into a mini multi song montage, which included the likings of AC/DC's *Highway to Hell*, Black Sabbath's *Iron Man* and Lynard Skynard's *Sweet Home Alabama*. During their ode to *Sweet Home Alabama*, they took the liberty to change the words around to "*Sweet Home Rochester-Buffalo!*"

Yet again, Green Day spoiled all the fun by playing some new song, but they soon made up for it by playing a huge chunk of awesome old school songs! I loved that they played stuff off of their *Dookie* album, including *When I Come Around, Longview, Basket Case,* and *She*. I have good memories of being in 5th grade at St. Stephen School and rocking out to that album.

Green Day played another great song, *King for a Day*.

Then Green Day went on another muilti-cover song montage, which included the Isley Brother's *Shout*, the Rolling Stone's *(I Can't Get No) Satisfaction,* and a few verses from the Beatles *Hey Jude*. While Green Day played *Shout*, a few die-hard fans sang the Buffalo Bills Shout song.

Green Day played another scrub song that Shannon and I didn't know, but they made up for it by playing *Minority*.

Green Day was trickey and convinced us that *Minority* was their closer, but they came back out for a much appreciated encore.

To start off their encore, Green Day played *American Idiot*. Considering all the covers and lyric changes to many songs that night, I was so hoping that Green Day would cover Weird Al Yankovick and play *Canadian Idiot*—but sadly, they did not.

Green Day continued with the encore by playing *Jesus of Suburbia*. They ended the night on another anticlimactic scrub song.

I enjoyed the show for the most part, though Green Day should have stuck with their old stuff. If I had my way, I would have hopped into the DeLorean time machine and gone back to the 1990s to see a Green Day show, possibly the Woodstock 94 show.

Once the concert was over, Shannon and I were hungry, so we went to Empire Hots for some trash plates. After late night munchies, it was bed time because we both had work the next morning. We were both old farts, working for the man and we couldn't sleep in like the kids we used to be.

90s Revival-Part II

It was the month of August in the year 2013AD.

Shannon was trolling the internet website of www.Groupon.com She saw that there were discounted tickets for Mark McGrath's 90's revival concert tour, Under the Sun Tour 2013. Shannon said Groupon was offering a BOGO deal.

I had no idea what "BOGO" was because I did not speak girl shopping lingo. Shannon informed me that "BOGO" stood for "buy one get one."

To that, I said, "Buy one, get one what?"

Shannon said, "Free."

I was confused. I asked, "If it's *'buy one get one free'* why don't they call it BOGOF?"

Shannon said, "I don't know. I didn't make up the word or acronym. Do you want to go?"

I told her that I did.

I won't lie, but I'm still stuck in the 1990s. It was a great decade to experience. The Buffalo Bills opened the 90s with "Wide Right" and the Buffalo Sabres closed out the 90s with "No Goal."

The 1990s were a wonderful time. It was a part of my innocent youth.

The 1990s were a time when music didn't suck! Nirvana was still alive, people still drove American cars, and the Buffalo Bills were good.

The 1990s were a time when people watched porn on VHS, not the internet…and for those precious few who had internet, it took forever to download a boobie picture of Pam Anderson over dial up internet. And it sucked when someone would call the house phone and kick you off the limited World Wide Web. The 1990s were a time when you were defined as a Sega or Nintendo kid; Team Sonic or Team Mario. I was a Sega kid. My Top 5 Sega games, in case you were wondering, were: NHL '94, Sonic 2, Golden Ax, Ristar, and Ninja Turtles (any title).

The 1990s were a time when the Teenage Mutant Ninja Turtles saved the day!

The 1990s were a time when Nickelodeon had Nicktoons; cartoons that didn't suck.

The 1990s were a time when MTV showed music videos and Beavis and Butthead.

Sadly, the 1990s were a time that will never happen again. The 1990s will be a time that I will remember being 6-15 years old.

Well that's enough reminiscing, time for the concert!

It was midafternoon on Saturday July 27, 2013 when Shannon and I hopped into our minivan to drive to CMAC in Canandaigua, NY.

As we waited in line to park, we saw a sign for $15 VIP parking. We figured that we would give VIP parking a shot.

It turned out that there was no line for VIP parking and that the parking lot was right next to the venue.

As soon as we parked the van, Shannon broke out a couple airplane bottles of vodka for us to drink on the way into the show.

I tried to drink the vodka, but it was just too painful. It was like drinking warm rubbing alcohol, it burned. I gave my baby bottle of vodka to Shannon.

Moments later, we had our $15 Groupon tickets scanned and we were in the venue!

Our first stop was to the beer kiosk. We each got a tall boy of Blue Light.

It turned out that our discounted bargain tickets were under the pavilion awning. As a matter of fact, we were about 15 or 20 rows away from the stage!

We watched the opening act play. Shannon asked me if I knew who they were, but I couldn't recognize any of their songs.

The opener played about 5 songs. When the band played their last song, *The Way*, I realized that we were watching Fast Ball. No wonder I didn't recognize any of their other songs, they were a one hit wonder.

Once Fast Ball finished their set, Mark McGrath came out and thanked Fast Ball for their performance. Once McGrath was done talking and left the stage Shannon and I got up to walk around. I noticed that my coworker Trevor was sitting in the row behind us. We went over to say hello and I introduced Shannon to him. Trevor introduced his wife and sister to us. It turned out that T-Dawg and Co. also took advantage of the Groupon offer.

Shannon and I wandered around the venue a little more. We could see why the concert tickets were on Groupon: because there were not many people there. We figured that the seats might fill in some more as the evening progressed.

Next on the playbill was Vertical Horizon. I had heard of Vertical Horizon, but I never got into them. Back in college, Shannon was into VH. I remember being on the Daemen College cross country team and teammates Shannon and Scott Tanski would often play VH.

Shannon really enjoyed seeing Vertical Horizon. She recognized most of their songs while I knew none. VH played about 8 songs for their set. Once Vertical Horizon finished their set, McGrath came out and thanked them and asked the crowd to clap for them again.

After Vertical Horizon finished playing, it was time to reload on beer!

But before we got beer, we had to drain the bladders.

Shannon came out of the latrine disgusted. She said the bathrooms were disgusting and looked as if they weren't cleaned at all.

Next, we made our way to the beer kiosk and reloaded on Labatt Blue Light. Shannon told me that one of her coworkers was there at the concert too, so we made our way over to find him.

Soon it was time to take our seats because McGrath was introducing the next band, Gin Blossoms.

I'm not 100% sure, but I think Gin Blossoms played the exact same set as they did the summer before at the Summerland Tour. They played their only radio hit that I knew of, *Hey Jealousy*. Gin Blossoms played about 8 other songs as well for their set. Once they were done playing, McGrath came back on stage to thank them and us for showing our support.

During the next set change, Shannon and I went over to talk to Trevor, his wife and sister.

Minutes later, McGrath took the stage with his band Sugar Ray.

Sugar Ray kicked off their set with a new song *Summertime's Coming*, which I had not heard before. Sugar Ray's second song was one that Shannon and I knew, *Someday*.

McGrath and company played another song I didn't know, but Shannon remembered it.

Sugar Ray then played a song that everyone knew, *Every Morning*.

In between songs, lead singer McGrath decided to take us on a stroll down memory lane. He told us how he and lead guitarist Rodney Sheppard formed the band 27 years ago (that's 1986 for you non-math gurus).

McGrath introduced the rest of the band to us too. Besides Rodney Sheppard on guitar, their drummer for the show was Dean Butterworth, formerly of the crappy band Good Charlotte. Butterworth was still dressed up in the Good Charlotte attire because he was wearing black slacks, a short sleeve collared button down dress shirt and a skinny red pencil tie. His look did not mesh well with the rest of the band's laid back California look. McGrath introduced the bassist, Serg Dmitrijevic.

After memory lane, Sugar Ray played some more songs including *When it's Over*.

Sheppard broke out an acoustic guitar and plucked out the opening chords to the Violent Femmes's *Blister in the Sun*. McGrath looked at Sheppard and said that the audience was too young to remember that song. Naturally the fans cheered because they did in fact know the tune. Sugar Ray's cover of *Blister in the Sun* was very good. I liked it when bands pulled off good cover tunes.

Sugar Ray ended their set with their biggest song, *Fly*.

After Sugar Ray finished playing Shannon and I had to pee again. Shannon refused to go back into the unclean bathrooms. I looked at the lawn section behind us and said, "Well, there doesn't look like there are many people in the lawn…and it's pretty dark out by the fence…and there's a big pine tree back there…"

Shannon said, "Um…let's go for a walk and check it out."

Shannon ended up peeing underneath the security blanket of protection underneath the big pine tree and it was one of the hottest things I've ever seen…that night.

By the time Shannon and I got back to our seats, it was time for the main event! McGrath came back out on stage to introduce the headliner for the evening, Smash Mouth! Smash Mouth opened with a cover of Question Mark and the Mysterians' *Can't Get Enough of You Baby*.

I didn't know the next couple songs that Smash Mouth played, but they sounded good.

While lead singer Steve Harwell was singing on stage, all I could think of was how much he reminded me of Mr. Toad in *The Wind in the Willows* by Kenneth Grahame. I think in life, most people look like cartoon characters; it's a fact, just look around.

Like the last four bands, Smash Mouth had a short set. However they did play their classic hit *Walkin' on the Sun.*

Smash Mouth spiced up their set with two more covers, the Kink's *You Really Got Me* and The Monkees' *I'm a Believer.* Both covers sounded great!

Smash Mouth closed their set with another one of their hits, *All Star.*

Once the show ended, Shannon and I said good bye to Trevor and company. Shannon and I made our way back to the minivan. We were both hungry so once again, we agreed upon garbage plates from Empire Hots!

Cornell Unplugged

I emailed my 88 year old Grandpa Ziggy, "Hi Grandpa, what are you doing Tuesday November 5th? Do you want to go with me to a concert and see Chris Cornell? He is playing at UB and it is an acoustic show. He's playing at the theater at UB so there will be assigned seats. I will even buy you dinner; Mighty Taco. It will be good for you to get out of the house."

Grandpa emailed me back, "I don't know who Chris Cornell is, but I will go to the concert with you."

Since Grandpa did not know who Chris Cornell was, I emailed Grandpa back, "Chris Cornell plays rock music. He was a part of the grunge revolution in Seattle in the early 1990s. He's the lead singer for Soundgarden, Temple of the Dog, and Audioslave. He also does solo work."

Grandpa replied back via email and said he would happy to accompany me.

Now a lot has happened since the last time I saw Chris Cornell. When I last saw him, he was performing by himself with a backup band at K-Rockathon in Weedsport, NY in 2007.

Since then, Chris Cornell and the rest of the boys from Soundgarden pulled a "Blues Brothers" and got the band back together. They released a double disc glorified greatest hits album, a live album, and a new album.

Soundgarden went on tour, but nowhere near Western New York. They did hit up Toronto a couple of times, but tickets were impossible to come by.

Chris Cornell's acoustic solo tour started right when Soundgarden's summer concert tours ended.

It was finally November 5, 2013. I got into work early so I could leave early and make it to the concert on time.

When I got out of work, I had to run home and let Teppo puppy out and feed him. Then Teppo and I hopped into my blue 2003 Dodge Caravan with 222,255 miles on her. Teppo and I made the hour and a half trip from Rochester to Buffalo.

I dropped Teppo off with my mom and picked up Grandpa Ziggy. Next stop, UB north campus!

Now, my only request was that I wanted to hear Chris Cornell play *Black Hole Sun*. When I saw Cornell at K-Rockathon, he jipped me and all the other concert goers by not playing *Black Hole Sun*.

I had been to UB a handful of times throughout the years, so I thought I knew where the performing arts center was. Well apparently I thought wrong. Every building in UB's campus looked the same, especially at night. It turned out that I parked pretty much on the opposite side of the campus. Also, it didn't help that the UB Bulls football team was playing a home game that night; it just complicated the parking situation.

It took Grandpa Ziggy and me about a half hour to walk our way to the performing arts center. During the entire walk, Grandpa pointed out empty parking spots, inquiring why we didn't park in the available spots. I told him that the walk and fresh air would do him well since he was cooped up in mom's house all day long; Grandpa needed his exercise anyway. Grandpa Ziggy complained during the entire walk on how far we had to walk. There were a couple times that I thought he was going to hit me with his cane!

We made it to the performing arts center by 7:30pm. It was good timing because the opener was about to take the stage.

I asked the ushers if there was an elevator up to the balcony and they said there was not one. I thought Grandpa was going to whack me with his cane when I told him we had to walk up the stairs, but instead he let out a, "Holy smokes!"

Thankfully we were not sitting at the last row in the balcony; our seats were four rows up. We got to our seats just as the opener Bhi Bhiman started his set.

Bhiman played a few original songs before playing a cover of Arlo Guthrie's *Coming into Los Angeles*. Bhiman's cover was pretty good.

Bhiman talked to us in between each of his songs. He said that he was excited to play and be on tour with Chris Cornell.

Bhiman played a few more song before ending his set with a cover. Bhiman instructed us that we were going to whistle the intro to his last song. Bhiman whistled the notes for us first, and then we followed and rehearsed a couple times. It turned out that we were whistling to the tune of the Dire Straits' *Walk of Life*. The whole whistling thing sounded pretty cool when the entire theater whistled in harmony with Bhiman's guitar playing and singing.

During Intermission, Grandpa Ziggy and I talked and solved all the world's problems. I asked him what he thought about the Buffalo Sabres trading away their captain Thomas Vanek. Grandpa thought that the Vanek trade to the NY Islanders was a good deal because in return, we got power forward Matt Moulson and two draft picks.

While talking to Grandpa, I spotted my old childhood neighbor that I grew up with! It was Lindsey Hahn and her husband Nick! I told Grandpa that I would be right back.

I ended up talking to Lindsey and Nick for about 5 or 10 minutes; catching up on things. I told Lindsey and Nick that I brought Grandpa Ziggy to the concert and they thought it was pretty awesome that he wanted to come.

I do have to say that I thought Grandpa Ziggy was the oldest person at the concert, 88 years old. I think Lindsey and I were possibly the youngest people there, 29 years old.

I eventually said good bye to Lindsey and Nick and returned to my seat next to Grandpa Ziggy.

Minutes later the lights went out, people cheered and Chris Cornell took the stage!

Cornell walked to the center of the stage and took a seat at the singular stool. The stool was on top of a very large oriental style rug. Behind the stool were about four or five acoustic guitars. To the left of the stage was a turn table.

Cornell acknowledged our cheers as he grabbed one of the acoustic guitars. Next he took a seat on the stool and said hi to us. He asked us how we were doing and everyone cheered! He told us that he couldn't remember the last time that he was in Buffalo and a couple fans yelled out a few different dates from the 1990s. Cornell told us that the 1990s were a blurry haze to him and that he didn't remember much from that decade.

Cornell said that it was great to be back in Buffalo and that he had a quick story for us. Right before he left his place in New York City, his wife asked him what city he was playing in that night. Cornell told his wife, "Buffalo." Cornell said his wife looked at him with shock and told him to wear a heavier coat because Buffalo was always freezing! Cornell told us that he got off the plane earlier that day and said that the weather was fine; it was in the 60s, which was abnormal for a November day in Buffalo. Cornell told us that as a kid, he remembered watching Vicks Vapor Rub commercials. He said the Vicks commercials would advertise that winter was coming and to stock up on Vicks with a screen shot of a blizzard in Buffalo.

Cornell's first song of the night was a solo song, *Scar on the Sky*.

For Cornell's second song, he gave us some background information to it. He said that after the 9-11 attacks on America, he supported President Bush's initiative on finding the evil that attacked America and bring them to justice. Cornell said he was not a fan of war and he did not like or support the invasion of Iraq. *Silence the Voices* were Cornell's thoughts about the situation.

Next, Cornell told us that a few years back he was asked to write the theme song for the James Bond movie *Casino Royale*. Cornell told us that he was honored to write and sing the song. Cornell said that not many artists had that on their resume, noting that former Beatle Paul McCartney also wrote a Bond theme song. Cornell added that he had never met McCartney. He did mention that the only other big rock legend that he had met was Dave Grohl. Cornell then played *You Know My Name* for us.

Then Cornell spiced things up by playing an Audioslave song that he wrote. Cornell said that *Dandelion* was a song written about his daughter. He went on to tell us that he wrote the song while his daughter was in his wife's stomach. Then he paused, and rephrased his statement, by saying the song was written while his daughter was in his wife's womb. Cornell said that he thought "stomach" was an ugly word and didn't know why people said that babies are in people stomachs. He said that when people say the babies are in people's stomachs, it sounded like people ate their babies. He added that womb sounds like a lovely word.

Dandelion was followed up by another Audioslave song, *Original Fire*. Cornell said *Original Fire* was about the feeling and atmosphere surrounding the Seattle music scene before the whole grunge revolution became main stream.

All throughout Cornell's set, in between songs, fans yelled out requests. I was hoping for fans to call out *Right Turn*, an Alice in Chains song that Cornell sang vocals on, but it was not requested. However, quite a few fans shouted out to hear *Sunshower*, a song that I hadn't heard of before. Cornell told us that he would play *Sunshower*, but before he did that, he told us a little story about the song. He said *Sunshower* was his first single after Soundgarden broke up in the late 90s. He said that *Sunshower* was not what big burly men who were Soundgarden fans were expecting. Cornell stopped, retracted, and said that not all Soundgarden fans were big burly men. He said that Soundgarden was a wonderful and beautiful thing and he wanted to leave Soundgarden intact and did not want to replicate it. *Sunshower* was a piece of work he could not have done in Soundgarden and it was a different way of him expressing himself.

Cornell told us he was going to play a Soundgarden song. I was hoping for *Black Hole Sun*, but instead he played *Halfway There*, a new song off Soundgarden's latest album *King Animal*.

Before playing his next song, Cornell said the final product was the fifth version of the song. He said he had trouble on whether the song should be slow or fast and what tempo and beat it should have. He said that he and Soundgarden recorded the song a few different ways before finding the right sound. Cornell then began to strum out the first opening chords to *Fell on Black Days* and the crowd enthusiastically cheered.

Cornell also played *Getaway Car*. The only comments about that song came when he finished playing it, and he informed us that it was an Audioslave song, but I already knew that.

Within the set list were a few songs that I didn't recognize, but I was just happy to see and hear Cornell perform. He did play an old classic that everyone knew, *The Day I Tried to Live*, a Soundgarden tune.

Cornell took a small break between songs to give us the inspiration and motivation for the next song. He said a while back, he was trying to play *One* from memory. He said he thought he knew most of the lyrics to the song, but when he tried singing it, he realized that he forgot more than he knew. He said he went on line and typed in "One lyrics" and clicked on the first link that came up. While reading the lyrics, he realized he was reading the lyrics from a different song of the same name. He commented that he liked both songs, so he decided to combine the two of them into one song. Cornell then played us his version of U2's and Metallica's *One*. I was not a fan of U2 let alone their song *One*, however I was a pretty big 'tallica fan and liked their song *One*. Cornell's rendition of the two songs was very good.

156

Cornell dedicated a song to his friend Natasha Schneider, who had passed away. Cornell spoke highly of Schneider, saying that she was a good friend and how she was a great piano player. Cornell told us that he was going to play a song off his solo album *Euphoria Morning* for Schneider. Cornell got up from his stool and walked over to the turn table to put a record on for the background music. Cornell told us that Schneider played the piano piece on *When I'm Down*, and with that, Cornell began to sing the song.

Cornell played *Wooden Jesus*, a Temple of the Dog song. It was a good song, but not my favorite Temple of the Dog song. I would have liked to hear a different one.

It was 10:30pm on the dot and Grandpa Ziggy looked at me and said, "Man this guy sings a lot! Well I'm ready. Let's go." And with that, Grandpa proceeded to get up. I didn't want to leave just then! There were still more songs to hear! I figured that there was at least another half hours' worth of show to go! I thought the show would have ended at 11pm at the earliest. I didn't want to miss out on more songs, but I knew Grandpa had had enough. I wasn't going to complain or argue with him. Come on, he agreed to go to an acoustic rock concert with me. I felt a little bad leaving the show early, but then again, Chris Cornell had already played for an hour and 45 minutes! That was longer than some other concerts I had been to.

I knew the real reason why Grandpa Ziggy wanted to leave, the Buffalo Sabres. That night the Sabres were playing on the West Coast. They were playing the San Jose Sharks and the game started at 10:30pm Eastern Standard Time. I figured Grandpa wanted to get back to mom's house at a reasonable hour and try to catch as much of the game before falling asleep; I didn't blame him.

As we left our seats, Chris Cornell brought back Bhi on stage to help him sing *Hunger Strike*; a song written by Cornell when he was in Temple of the Dog. *Hunger Strike* was probably my favorite Temple of the Dog songs, let alone Cornell songs. The crowd also loved the song since they all cheered and clapped when they heard the opening notes.

Grandpa and I got to the main doors of the performing arts center and I told him to sit on the bench and I would run back to get the car for him. I didn't want him to walk that long distance again.

On the ride back to mom's house, I put the Sabres game on the radio. Grandpa told me he had fun and "enjoyed the banjo player." He said he never grew up with that kind of music in Poland. He was used to ball room dance and waltz music.

I had Grandpa back to mom's house before 11pm, with plenty of time left for Grandpa to catch the rest of the 1st Period of the Sabres game.

It was a little after 11:30pm when Teppo puppy and I hit the road back to Rochester. Teppo and I made a quick pit stop to the Mighty Taco on Grand Island. I ordered a couple three cheese nacho burritos and a Loganberry beverage!

Teppo and I got back to our house by 1am.

The UB Bulls football team had beaten Ohio Bobcats 30-3 on ESPN2.

The Buffalo Sabres had beaten the San Jose Sharks in the Shark Tank 5-4 in a shootout!

At the end of the day, I still did not hear Chris Cornell sing *Black Hole Sun*. As a true Buffalonian, the only thing I could say about that was, "*Maybe next time…*"

Hootie

For Christmas of 2013, I surprised Shannon with a pair of tickets to see Darius Rucker in concert at Turning Stone Casino in Verona, New York.

Everybody knows Darius because he used to be the former front man of Hootie and the Blowfish.

I had never seen Hootie and the Blowfish or Darius Rucker solo before.

Shannon saw Hootie and the Blowfish back in 2006 at the Erie Basin Marina in downtown Buffalo. She and her family enjoyed the concert, but Shannon noted that a few songs they played were a little twangy, which was not Hootie and the Blowfish's style.

Since Shannon saw them, Hootie and the Blowfish disbanded and Darius Rucker went on a country solo career.

It was Saturday morning, February 15, 2014. Shannon and I had our tickets for the show, but we still needed to find lodging for the night.

I went on Orbitz.com and located a Days Inn in Rome, NY. The Days Inn was also a pet friendly motel, so we could bring our puppy-dog Teppo Numminen.

Our goal was to leave Rochester by noon, drive the 2 ½ hours to Rome, check into the motel, and get to the casino by 3pm and get some gambling in before the concert. Shannon and I didn't want to gamble after the show because Turning Stone gets packed after events let out. For instance, the previous year, Shannon and I saw ESPN Friday night boxing at Turning Stone. The festivities started at 7pm and ended after 11pm. Once boxing ended, we tried to do some gambling, but every slot machine was occupied and you couldn't even squeeze up to a table game. So we tried to stick to our game plan, but we left late.

We got to Days Inn by 3:30pm. There were no issues checking in. I told the front desk that I had a dog with me. I was charged an additional $25 for Teppo.

Shannon, Teppo, and I checked into our room and unloaded our bags. Teppo seemed to approve of the room. He liked that there were two queen beds.

I filled up Teppo's water bowl and food bowl. Shannon and I read Teppo the riot act and told him that me needed to be on his best behavior. We brought a bunch of his toys for him to play with. Also, we left the TV on for him, just in case he wanted to watch Full House.

It was 4pm when we stepped foot onto the gaming floor at Turning Stone and it was already busy.

Shannon and I grabbed a round of beers at a bar.

Turning Stone was not my favorite casino for a few reasons. First of all, beer was not complimentary. Turning Stone was an 18 and up casino so they did not serve free adult beverages. Secondly, the place smelled of tobacco smoke. There was such a haze that Jason Voorhees could cut through it with his machete. Lastly, I never had any good luck at Turning Stone.

I played some roulette and lost my $30.

I played Beat the Dealer, a dice game. It was $2 a hand. I eventually lost $6.

I watched some people play a spinning wheel game. It was a good thing I didn't play because every spot I would have bet on never came up.

It was quarter to 7 when Shannon and I left the gaming floor and we made our way to the event center.

After getting our tickets scanned, we grabbed a round of Labatt Blues and then found our seats in the balcony.

Our balcony seats were the same price as the seats on the floor, but I preferred the bird's eye view. Also, Shannon suffered from Short Person Syndrome. I didn't want to get floor seats because we inevitably get stuck behind a tall person. Instead our balcony seats were aisle seats in the last row of our section and they were nice seats.

The opening act was David Nail. I wasn't into country nor western music. To me, David Nail played typical sounding country music. David Nail was alright to listen to, but the volume coming out of the speakers was quite loud. I had a beer in hand, so life was good, and so was the eye candy.

The Darius Rucker's 2014 True Believer's Tour was the first country music show I had been to. I had heard many good things about the quality and caliber of eye candy at country shows…girls in cow boys boots, tight skirts, tight fitting jeans, flannel shirts with the right amount of cleavage, long curly hair, and an occasional cowboy hat. All the stories were true! The eye candy at the country show was so much better than say the lack of eye candy at a Pearl Jam show…different kind of jeans and different form fitting flannel.

The second act was Eli Young Band, who I never heard of before. I did not like the way they sounded. The speakers were cranked so loud that their music was too distorted. I felt like David Nail should have gone back on stage.

During Eli Young Band's set, I had to pee and grab more beer. Shannon was hungry so I was going to grab her a pretzel too.

After peeing and washing my hands with soap, water, and friction for 30 seconds, I walked over to the concession line. I ended up buying two Blues, two pretzels, and a popcorn. I quickly realized that I could not make it back to my seat without dropping something.

Instead, I placed the beers and food down on the window ledge. Then I grabbed my phone and texted Shannon that I needed help with the beers and food. Shannon wasn't too into Eli Young Band, so she texted that she would be down soon.

While I waited for Shannon, I watched a few minutes of the Syracuse Orangemen's basketball game. The undefeated and #1 ranked Orangemen were hosting unranked North Carolina State Wolfpack at the Carrier Dome.

Apparently there were a lot of people who didn't care for Eli Young Band because there were at least 50 people huddled around the TV next to me. There was another TV on the other side of the event center and there were at least 50 guys around that TV too!

Moments later Shannon arrived. We ate our pretzels and watched a part of the Orange game. As soon as we finished our pretzels, we decided to make our way back to our seats. Just then, Eli Young Band's set finished and all the concert goers flooded into the concession stand area and flocked to the TV to catch the final minutes of the 'Cuse game.

Soon Shannon and I were back at our seats and ready for Hootie to take the stage!

Before Darius could take the stage, we had to wait for the roadies to finish the set change.

Eventually the house light went out and the entire event center was dark. People started to cheer and Darius Rucker and his five piece band took the stage. He was lead vocals and guitar. There was another guitarist, steel guitarist, bassist, drummer, fiddler, and keyboardist.

I had not heard much of Darius' country stuff; I only knew his Hootie material. So I had to rely on Shannon to tell me what songs they were playing.

I did not know Darius' opening song but it was a country tune, though it may have been *Radio*. I didn't mind the song because the video background showed a Chevy Chevelle driving along.

Darius played some more country songs including his chart topping hits *Come Back Song, This,* and *Alright*.

Before he played *Don't Think I Don't Think About It*, he said that it was his first country hit single. He thanked his fans and country music and then played the song.

Darius told us that he was going to play the first country song he ever wrote...he soon began to play the opening chords to Hootie and the Blowfish's *Time*. I had no idea that *Time* was a country tune, but hearing it with the steel guitar made it sound very country.

Darius followed up *Time* with a cover of John Cougar Mellencamp's *Pink Houses*. I enjoyed Darius' rendition better than John Cougar's original.

Another song Darius and his band played was *Drinkin' and Dialin'*. It was a funny song because it was so true! So many of us have thought it was a good idea to use the phone after a few drinks. *Drinkin' and Dialin'* brought to light the entertainment and stupidity of it.

In between songs, Darius asked us how we were doing. Of course every one cheered. Darius then asked, "Did Syracuse win the basketball game?!" The entire event center went wild and cheered. Darius said he would take that as a "Yes." Syracuse beat NC State 56-55 in a nail biter.

Darius played a couple other Hootie songs, which made me happy. Darius played *Let Her Cry, Hold My Hand,* and *Only Wanna Be With You.*

He played some more original country tunes before closing out the show with two covers: Old Crow Medicine Show's *Wagon Wheel* and then ended the night with Prince's *Purple Rain.*

And like that, the show was over.

Shannon and I were seated right next to an exit, so we made a mad dash to beat the large crowd. Shannon wanted to play some video poker. I told her I would grab us another round of Blue.

The first bar I went to was four people deep and the drinks were flowing like molasses. I found a different bar with no line. I got my two Blues, tipped my bartender, and then found Shannon at video poker.

To the left of Shannon was some old hag smoking a Vagina Slims cigarette and to the right of Shannon was some bum smoking a Philly blunt. The second hand smoke was choking Shannon out. We quickly left and finished our beers elsewhere.

Shannon and I were hungry, and we did not want to dine at the casino. We remembered that our motel had a Denny's at it. Shannon and I agreed upon Denny's for midnight munchies.

After having breakfast at Denny's, Shannon and I went back to our room where Mr. Teppo greeted us. Teppo was quite happy to see us.

Earlier, I had asked Shannon whether she thought Teppo would sleep on our bed or the other queen bed in the room. Shannon and I both thought Teppo would sleep on our bed because he was a huge baby.

To our surprise, Teppo slept on the other queen bed. He had the entire bed to sprawl out on.

The next morning, I showed Teppo how much fun it was to jump from bed to bed. Teppo thought it was awesome as he chased me bed to bed!

The Goos

Up until Friday August 22, 2014, I had considered myself a bad Buffalonian because I had never seen Buffalo's own, the Goo Goo Dolls.

I had a chance to see the Goo Goo Dolls perform for free in downtown Buffalo at City Hall on July 4, 2004, but I passed up that opportunity, and have regretted it ever since.

You see, back in 2004 I was a broke college student working maintenance at Beaver Island State Park, making about $7.15 an hour. Since the 4th of July was a holiday, I got holiday pay, which was the equivalent to time and a half. Additionally, the 4th was always a busy day at the park, so I was working past my scheduled 8 hours. On average, I would work 10-12 hours on the 4th, so it was well worth my time to be at work, making money.

Besides being a broke college student, I had just bought a 1980 Chevrolet Camaro Z28! When I bought the car, the engine had just had a fire, so the car needed a full restoration, which I was eager to take on!

From a logical and monetary stand point, it was wiser for me to work than to get drunk in downtown Buffalo the Goo Goo Dolls concert.

Fast forward 10 years later, I was going to finally see the Goo Goo Dolls! Shannon's friend Brigid found a Groupon for the Goo Goo Dolls show at Darien Lake Performing Arts Center; discounted tickets were only $20.

Brigid and Shannon met me at work a little after 4:30pm. The three of us carpooled from my work to Darien Lake.

We hopped on the 90 in Henrietta and drove eastbound towards Buffalo. We got off at the Batavia exit because we were going to take the secret Batmobile route into Darien Lake; we wanted to bypass any concert traffic there may have been.

Once we got to Darien Lake Amusement Park and Performing Arts Center, we had to sit in a line of cars. Park staff had to direct the concert traffic to a different parking lot than the amusement park traffic; that was a cluster f.

Minutes later, parking attendants directed us where to park. As soon as we parked the minivan, we were swarmed by a few dudes hustling bootleg/counterfeit concert shirts. Brigid, Shannon and I did not want any. Darien Lake Security and New York State Troopers were patrolling the parking lot and saw the hustlers, but didn't kick them out; Brigid, Shannon and I thought that was weird. Maybe the hustlers paid off the authorities.

After the riff raff left, it was time to pop the tail gate to the minivan and have dinner and pregame before the show!

Shannon had a half day of work, so when she got out of work, she went shopping for food at Wegmans for us. For the record, Wegmans was (and is) the best grocery store in the world; it is the Walt Disney World of grocery stores! Shannon got Chinese food and sangria for Brigid and subs for us. Shannon had a NA beer because she was pregnant. She got me a 24 ounce can of Labatt Ice.

While we ate dinner, the opening act, Plain White T's, took the stage. The three of us had no interest in seeing Plain White T's, especially me. I did not want to be tortured with their first "hit" song, *Hey There Delilah*. Brigid and Shannon told me Plain White T's had another song that the radio was trying to pump.

Thankfully Plain White T's only played for about a half hour.

After we finished dinner, the three of us continued to tail gate.

A short while later, we could hear Daughtry take the stage.

I wasn't a fan of Daughtry. The only thing I knew about him and his band was that he was a contestant on an annoying TV singing talent show.

Brigid, Shannon and I shot the shit for a bit before deciding to head into the venue.

Once inside the venue, the three of us had to pee, so we went to the bathroom.

Next we walked out to the lawn and found a nice spot, smack dab in the middle to lay out our blanket.

For the next half hour or 40 minutes, we had to suffer through Daughtry's music, which I was not a fan of. He's probably a nice guy, but he seemed a little douchey on stage. In between songs, he tried to pump up the crowd and told us all to get up and cheer. And then he would shriek into the microphone, which rang through everyone's ears.

Daughtry played the only song of his the I recognized, *It's All Over*. Unfortunately, his set was not all over, he still had more songs to sing! I was so bored during Daughtry's set that I went to the bathroom again to kill some time.

Brigid, Shannon and I were amazed that Daughtry was still playing. He started his set while the three of us were still tailgating. The only reason why we ventured into the venue was because we thought his set was ending soon. We were at the van for a good half hour before heading in. The walk in was about 10 minutes, then we had to pee and found a nice spot to sit on the lawn, which all took a lot of time.

Brigid, Shannon and I tried to kill some time during Daughtry's set by thinking up one song that we would like to hear the Goo Goo Dolls play. Brigid wanted to hear the Goos play *Broadway*. Shannon wasn't good with song titles; she just knew songs when she heard them, so her vote was for anything she recognized. I wanted to hear *Long Way Down* because it was a kick ass fast tune off their album *A Boy Named Goo*.

Thinking about our favorite Goo Goo Dolls songs only killed about a minute or two of time. Then it was back to reality as we suffered through more of Daughtry's shrieking.

It felt like an eternity, but Daughtry finally played his last song! Once he finished, I cheered really loudly. I quickly stopped cheering because I didn't want Daughtry to think he needed to come back out for an encore!

During the set change Shannon asked me if I wanted a beer. I thought about it for a moment and decided against it. I wasn't sure if it was a sign of maturity or me being cheap. I knew that I didn't need another beer because I still had to drive home, and according to New York State law, booze cruizin' was illegal. Secondly, I didn't want to pay for an overpriced beer.

It was around 9pm when a smoke machine poured a misty haze across the stage. Soon the stage lights were turned off and fans began to cheer.

The Goos came out on stage and began to play *Dizzy* and instantly the crowd cheered louder. *Dizzy* was followed up by *Big Machine*. The Goo's third song of the night was another fan favorite, *Slide*.

Then the Goo Goo Dolls played a few songs that I didn't know. Now I won't bull shit you and pretend to be Buffalo's biggest

Goos fan. That award would probably go to my old neighbor from South Central Grand Island Ryan Sherman.

As kids, Ryan and my older sister Sarah were thick as thieves, best friends. One of the biggest things they had in common was that they both loved the Goo Goo Dolls, though I felt that Ryan liked the Goos a little more.

Anywho, as a kid, I never needed to buy a Goo Goo Dolls album because Sarah and Ryan had everything in the Goos discography from albums to live recordings and singles to b sides. Whether or not I wanted to hear it, I still heard all the Goo's early stuff.

My sister Sarah was not at the show with us, but I was texting her what songs the Goos were playing. However, Ryan was at the show, but I had no idea where she was sitting.

Bassist Robbie Goo (as Sarah and Ryan called him) took a minute to talk to us. He said that it was great to be back home. He mentioned that for years the Goo Goo Dolls had meet and greet sessions before their concerts. He said that he really enjoyed the experience of meeting his fans. He added that recently, he and Johnny Goo had been meeting second generation Goo Goo Dolls fans and he thought that was awesome and very special. Robbie Goo dedicated the next song to all the second generation Goos fans. Brigid leaned over to Shannon's baby bump and said, "He's dedicating that song to you Baby DeRose!" Robbie Goo and the rest of the band began to play *Another Second Time Around.*

After the Goo Goo Dolls finished *Another Second Time Around* lead singer and guitarist Johnny Goo talked to us. He built upon Robbie Goo's thoughts about meeting fans before their shows. Johnny Goo said that there was one time at a meet and greet when he met a married couple. The wife whispered into Johnny Goo's ear and said that he was her freebie; a hall pass. Johnny Goo didn't know what to say and he was a little shocked and honored. Johnny Goo looked at the husband. The husband looked at Johnny Goo and knew what his wife told Johnny Goo. Johnny Goo said that the husband was nodding his head yes as he mouthed, "Oh yea!"

Johnny Goo went on to tell us that he called his wife to tell her about what he had experienced. Johnny Goo asked his wife who was on her freebie list. Mrs. Johnny Goo said that she liked some Latino singer. She then asked Johnny Goo who was on his list.

Johnny Goo said that he liked the red head down at the grocery store! He then told us he loved his wife and the Goo Goo Dolls then played *Come to Me*.

The Goos then slowed it down a little and played *Black Balloon*. The stage went dark and bright white and blue lights illuminated the stage and audience. During the song, a lot of fans inflated black balloons and began to hit them around like beach balls.

Black Balloon was followed up by another Goo hit, *Stay With You*.

The Goo Goo Dolls went on to play a few more tunes. During their set, Johnny Goo talked to us again. He said that it always felt great coming home and playing for his hometown fans because he felt that the fans actually cared and gave a shit. Johnny Goo added that he had a special treat for us that night. He said that they were going to play a brand new, unreleased song for us, but he never revealed the song's name. I enjoyed the song, it was typical Goo sounding (A couple months later I saw Ryan at Shannon's baby shower. I asked Ryan how she liked the Goos' concert. She said she really enjoyed it. I also asked her about the Goos' mystery song. Ryan informed me that the mystery song was *Caught in the Storm*, and it was going to be their next single off their latest album *Magnetic*).

In between songs, some fan yelled up to Johnny Goo that it was her 50th time seeing the Goo Goo Dolls. Johnny Goo congratulated her and said that it was his 9,000[th] time seeing the Goos perform and the fans laughed.

The Goos then kicked it old school by playing *Naked* and *Name*. The audience loved it as they all cheered. I was hoping that the Goos were going to keep with the *A Boy Named Goo* theme and play *Long Way Down*, but sadly they didn't. Instead they played a couple songs that I didn't know, including a song where Robbie Goo sang again. Shannon wasn't a hug fan of Robbie Goo's singing because he sounded like a Muppet. Shannon was perplexed because even though she was a huge Muppets fan, she didn't want to hear Robbie sing. Shannon wanted Robbie Goo to sing *Man or Muppet* from Disney's 2011 movie *The Muppets*, but that didn't happen either.

The Goo Goo Dolls did play *Better Days* which was a song that was occasionally played at HSBC Arena before Buffalo Sabre games.

Next the Goos played another song I didn't know, but followed it up with *Broadway*. Brigid and the rest of the audience cheered and applauded with joy.

Lastly, the Goo Goo Dolls ended their set with *Iris*, a song written for the *City of Angels* movie starring Meg Ryan and that fartknocker "actor" Nick Cage. I felt Nick Cage's acting talent rivaled that of Keanu Reeves in that I wasn't sure which was the worst actor in Hollywood.

Anyway, the Goos played *Iris*, another fan favorite and hit. The fans sang along with Johnny Goo.

After *Iris* the music stopped. The Goo Goo Dolls left the stage. It seemed as if the show was over, but the house lights were not turned on. Fans still hung around and cheered, hoping for an encore. A few moments went by before Johnny Goo came back out on stage and asked us fans if we knew that they were coming back out for an encore. The fans delightfully cheered.

The Goos started their encore with *Sympathy*.

The Goos' encore was only two songs long. They finished the evening off with a cover of Supertramp's *Give a Little Bit*.

At the conclusion of the Goos' set, Brigid, Shannon and I made a mad dash towards the exits in the back of the lawn section. The three of us rushed through the grassy parking lot to the minivan. We were trying to get the hell out of there in a hurry because leaving Darien Lake after a concert was a nightmare. We've heard horror stories on how it took people several hours just to leave the parking lot!

Thankfully we only waited in traffic for five or so minutes.

Before we got to Batavia, Shannon was falling asleep at the wheel. She asked if I would take over when we got to Batavia and I told her I would.

From Batavia to Henrietta, Shannon and Brigid were passed out.

Eventually we arrived back at my work. Brigid hopped in her car and drove home. By the time Shannon and I got back home it was 12:15am! Long day, good concert. I was finally able to cross the Goos off my "Need to See" concert list.

The Closer (Epilogue)

I've been to a lot of shows and concerts through the years. I know some of you reading this may complain that there were too many Foo Fighters stories in my book. I would have to agree with you, but I do have to say that the Foo Fighters were one of the best rock bands of the 1990s, but the *BEST* band of the 2000s.

I've seen Earth Crisis play at the Mohawk Place in downtown Buffalo, Niagara Falls' own Stemm open for Godsmack at Shea's Performing Arts Center, the Trews at Cozumel Grill & Tequila Bar, and Switchfoot at Sphere nightclub. I also saw Three Days Grace, Bad Religion, Slipknot, Papa Roach, Good Charlotte, Dropkick Murphys, Flogging Molly, Nickelback (though I don't like to admit it), and countless other bands that played at Buffalo's Thursday in the Square, Rochester's Lilac Festival, the Vans Warped Tour and Edgefest. All those shows were good, but they weren't as memorable as the concerts I told you about.

I also saw Eddie Money, Three Dog Night, Motley Crue, Kiss, Aerosmith, .38 Special, Alice Cooper, Bob Dylan, America, Queen + Paul Rodgers, and other old farts, but they weren't my generation. It was good to say that I've seen them in concert but it's not a part of my makeup or youth.

Like with almost every love affair, there was always the "one that got away." We already know that Nirvana is on the top of my list of bands I never saw (though I did get to see Dave Grohl, Kirst Novoselic, and Pat Smear perform together at a Foo Fighters show in Buffalo on the 20th anniversary of the release of Nirvana's *Nevermind*, but that's a story for another time). Also on the list are the Red Hot Chili Peppers, the Smashing Pumpkins, Rage Against the Machine, and a couple others…

There were a couple times that the Chili Peppers played in Toronto. The first time was September of 2006. At the time, I was a broke college student. The Chili Peppers were playing two shows at the Air Canada Centre. The shows were on a Monday and Tuesday. Shannon and I were back at college and we had cross country practice. Late afternoon classes and cross country practices made it almost impossible to make it up to Toronto for either shoe. In 2012 RHCP play another two day show at the ACC. For some reason, Shannon and I were busy that weekend.

At the start of my concert going career, the Smashing Pumpkins had broken up. Lead singer and guitarist Billy Corgan created a new band, Zwan, which was a bit of a super group. Zwan was playing at Alumni Arena at UB in Amherst in April of 2003. I was on the fence about going to the show but when I heard that Zwan would not be playing any Smashing Pumpkins tunes, I decided not to go. Apparently Zwan was only going to be playing songs off their debut album *Mary Star of the Sea.*

I never got the chance to see Rage Against the Machine because they broke up while I was still in high school.

After the breakup, the former members of RATM (minus lead singer Zack de la Rocha) teamed up with Soundgarden's lead singer Chris Cornel to for Audioslave.

Audioslave's first Canadian gig was in May of 2003 at the Kool Haus in Toronto. I wanted to go to the show, but I had no one to go with me. I asked my buddies and almost everyone at school but it seemed like everyone was busy or had an excuse.

I had an opportunity to see Aaron Lewis from Staind at UB back in 2007 but for some reason that I can't remember, I passed on the show. I heard it was a very good acoustic show where he played Staind songs and covers.

Jane's Addiction played at Darien Lake in 2013 but I passed on it because Darien Lake's concert parking situation is a cluster-f.

I thought Sublime was alright. Since the lead singer's death, the band reunited and began touring as Sublime with Rome. Sublime with Rome has come to Western New York several times throughout past few years, but I just never had the itch to see them.

As 2014 comes to a close, one chapter in my life ends and another is about to open. Baby DeRose is due to be born February 2, 2015. I've been told my life will change forever. I'm pretty sure that my rock concert days are pretty much coming to an end, or at least put on hiatus. I imagine that as soon as my kid(s) is(are) old enough to go to concerts, my bands that I paid top dollar to see will probably be all washed up and resorting to play free local festivals like Rochester's Lilac Festival, Buffalo's Thursday in the Square, shows at Artpark in Lewiston, or free casino shows.

With the dawn of kids on the horizon, I know that my future holds concert performances to the liking of school Christmas pageants, Sesame Street Live, and Disney on Ice.

Speaking about Disney on Ice, back in 2013 Shannon and I did a recon and went to Disney on Ice with my buddy Jeff and his wife Elissa. At the time, neither of us had kids, but we thought it was a cool thing to do on a Thursday night in January.

I'm not going to lie, but I thought Disney on Ice was pretty cool. First of all, there was no line for beer! Jeff, Elissa, Shannon, and I were pretty much the only adults drinking beer. All the fathers at the show stared at our beers and began to salivate, just like their little petri dish children as they stared at the jumbo bags of cotton candy.

The other cool think about Disney on Ice was the skating! Don't get me wrong, I'm not some dude who peaks at the urinals and likes figure skating. What I'm trying to say is that the show should have been called Disney Erotica on Ice!

During Disney Erotica on Ice, the skaters reenacted the Little Mermaid. After Ariel was transformed into a human, she skated around the ice with Prince Eric. Prince Eric picked up Ariel. She wrapped her long legs around Prince Eric as he mounted her from behind as they skated around in circles…it was hot. It was like a Disney fantasy come true!

The Erotica was spread amongst other Disney fairy tales too! Cinderella came out in her big blue ball gown and skated around the ice. As soon as Prince Charming entered the rink, Cinderella tore off her ball gown and skated around in a skimpy and very revealing skirt. *Boinggggg!* Cinderella and Prince Charming met at center ice and skated around for a bit before Prince Charming picked up Cinderella and flipped her upside down! The two for them skated around in the 69 position!

Even Belle and Beast had some sex-capades too! Beast hoisted Belle up and held her by the kooch as they skated around. I thought it would have been the icing on the cake if Beast spun Belle around like a basketball, but he did not.

I had no idea that Disney on Ice was so sexually provocative! If my kid(s) and Shannon want to go to Disney on Ice the next time it comes back to town, I have no problem!

The rock concert chapter is coming to an end. The chapter of fatherhood and child geared entertainment is about to begin. I am not signing off, but what I am saying is stay tuned…

Adam DeRose, December 31, 2014